GERTRUDE STEIN
AND THE PRESENT

GERTRUDE STEIN AND THE PRESENT

Allegra Stewart

HARVARD UNIVERSITY PRESS
Cambridge · Massachusetts
1967

FOR MY SISTER LUCILLE
with affection and gratitude

PREFACE

This book is focused upon the underlying experience of contemplation and creative dissociation which seems to me to
have determined not only Gertrude Stein's metaphysical
outlook but also her poetic practices and purposes. It must
be conceded that there is much in Gertrude Stein's life,
writing, and personality to suggest the jester as well as the
sage. Nevertheless, there is a profound underlying harmony
between the search for the "new word" which inspired, for
example, *Tender Buttons* and the philosophical views which
become explicit in *The Geographical History of America.*
It is a harmony between principle and application that cannot have evolved arbitrarily. It argues a deep experience of
some sort, and it is my conviction that this was the psychological experience of deep concentration, self-realization, or
"ingatheredness." Once having found this unity, I have had
to take it seriously—in spite of the apparently ordinary ideas
and the elements of triviality or frivolity in much of her
writing—as a long-neglected clue to the meaning of Gertrude
Stein's life and work as a whole.

Gertrude Stein, however, always denied any belief in God,
the God of the Bible and Western tradition, at least: she
seems to have regarded whatever breakthrough she made to
her own buried resources as an act of aesthetic creation rather
than of religious mysticism. For these reasons she is singularly akin to the twentieth-century spirit as a whole—to the
spirit, that is, of the creative minority. For the same reasons

it has been easiest to attack the problem first of all by way of Stein's philosophical ideas. Thus in Chapter One, "Stein and Her Era," I point out her affinities, personal and intellectual, with some of the important philosophers of her own time as well as such earlier men as James and Santayana, Bergson and Whitehead. In Chapter Two, "Language and Vision," I continue the discussion by pointing out the crucial importance, in several contexts, of the moment of dissociation. This point of "unhooking," at which the links between past determining factors and the future are temporarily loosened, was capable of leading, Gertrude Stein thought, to the emergence of new forms in the cosmic process or, in man's experience, to a state of enlarged consciousness.

This general explanation is followed by a detailed analysis in my third chapter of *Tender Buttons* as a verbal mandala— a work formed, I believe, by repeated acts of genuine concentration in the attempt to discover fresh language and to effect a breakthrough to deeper creativity. Many years later, after much work and an inevitable period of aridity and despair, Stein was to write *Doctor Faustus Lights the Lights*. This odd opera libretto is in subject matter devoted to those Jungian archetypes of self-realization and self-creation which are suggested in veiled fashion in *Tender Buttons*.

It is possible to see, in the curve of Gertrude Stein's life, an effort to counter the naturalistic vision of the cosmos as a purposeless process (a vision she accepted) with a vision of possibility and creativity. Perhaps this effort is most beautifully expressed in a passage from "England": "Anything that is everything and everything that is anywhere and everything that is everywhere has no special singular purpose. If purpose is intellectual then there is a garden, if there is a garden there is a fountain, if there is a fountain then there is an intellectual purpose."

I wish to express my appreciation to Butler University for a sabbatical leave and a faculty fellowship which enabled me to make a study of the vocabulary of *Tender Buttons*. In greatly altered form, a small part of the material in Chapter Five appeared in "The Quality of Gertrude Stein's Creativity," *American Literature*, January 1957. For their thoughtful reading of my manuscript and for their helpful suggestions, my gratitude goes to Harold Watts, Donald Sutherland, and William Alfred. I am more deeply indebted than I know how to say to Rebecca Pitts, who listened to these chapters as they were written and with whom I discussed endlessly the ideas on religion, philosophy, and the arts with which this book is concerned. My thanks go also to Joyce Lebowitz of Harvard University Press for her encouragement and guidance.

Quotations from Stein's *The Geographical History of America, Everybody's Autobiography, Lectures in America,* and *Wars I Have Seen* are copyright and reprinted by permission of Random House, Inc. The epigraph to Chapter Two is from *The Wisdom of Laotse,* translated and edited by Lin Yutang (New York: Modern Library, 1948). Grateful acknowledgment is made to the Estate of Gertrude Stein for permission to quote from various writings of Stein's, including *Tender Buttons* and *Doctor Faustus Lights the Lights.*

A. S.

December 1966
Indianapolis, Indiana

CONTENTS

ABBREVIATIONS OF STEIN TITLES

ABT   *The Autobiography of Alice B. Toklas.* New York: Harcourt, Brace and Company, 1933.

E   "An Elucidation." *Transition,* supplement, April 1927.

EA   *Everybody's Autobiography.* New York: Random House, 1937.

FIA   *Four in America.* Introduction by Thornton Wilder. New Haven: Yale University Press, 1947.

GHA   *The Geographical History of America, or the Relation of Human Nature to the Human Mind.* Introduction by Thornton Wilder. New York: Random House, 1936.

HTW   *How To Write.* Paris: Plain Edition, 1931.

LIA   *Lectures in America.* New York: Random House, 1935.

LOAP   *Last Operas and Plays.* Edited by Carl Van Vechten. New York, Toronto: Rinehart and Company, 1949.

MOA   *The Making of Americans.* Preface by Bernard Fay. New York: Harcourt, Brace and Company, 1934.

N   *Narration.* Introduction by Thornton Wilder. Chicago: University of Chicago Press, 1935.

P   *Picasso.* London: B. T. Batsford, Ltd., 1938.

TB   *Tender Buttons.* New York: Claire Marie, 1914 (Reprinted in *Selected Writings of Gertrude Stein.* Edited by Carl Van Vechten. New York: Random House, 1946.)

UK   *Useful Knowledge.* New York: Payson and Clarke, Ltd., 1928.

WAM   *What Are Masterpieces and Why Are There So Few of Them.* Introduction by Robert Bartlett Haas. Los Angeles: Conference Press, 1940.

WIHS   *Wars I Have Seen.* New York: Random House, 1944.

GERTRUDE STEIN
AND THE PRESENT

Hundreds of writers may be found in every long-civilized nation who for a short time believe and make others believe that they see and utter truths, who do not of themselves clothe one thought in its natural garment, but who feed unconsciously on the language created by the primary writers of the country, those, namely, who hold primarily on nature.
—*Emerson,* Nature

The care with which the rain is wrong and the green is wrong and the white is wrong, the care with which there is a chair and plenty of breathing. The care with which there is incredible justice and likeness, all this makes a magnificent asparagus, and also a fountain.
—*Gertrude Stein,* Tender Buttons

I. STEIN AND HER ERA

Certain European philosophers (especially Martin Heidegger, Gabriel Marcel, and, in a way, Max Picard) have attracted the attention of many Americans to a very significant tendency in contemporary art and thought. I do not allude to existentialism as such—rather, to a kind of inchoate effort (in which, of course, the literary existentialists play a conspicuous role) to bring about a rapprochement between philosophy on the one hand and language and literature on the other. Marcel, for example, in his preface to Picard's *World of Silence*, comments on the "value for ontology" of human language, referring especially in this connection to Heidegger's "Letter on Humanism." In the same preface Marcel says that today the philosopher "tends to draw nearer to the poet" and that the "unity which thought, as such, and poetry, as such, had in their beginnings is being recreated." [1]

The American reader of such words might well question whether recent writers and thinkers in this country have shown any tendency to "draw nearer" to one another. Regardless of what the philosophers have been doing, certainly most of the talented American writers of this century have not been notable for their power of thought. The tradition of the artist-philosopher has not been much respected: at least one hesitates to mention anyone in this connection except Eliot, and perhaps Pound. Indeed a certain intellectual innocence, or irrationality, or downright anti-intellectualism, was probably the dominant attitude of such figures as Sherwood Anderson, Scott Fitzgerald, and Hemingway—

1. Max Picard, *The World of Silence* (Chicago: Henry Regnery Company, 1952), pp. 9, 13.

all of whom expressed their time with considerable talent and integrity.

In the literary background of our era, however, stands the solitary and rather enigmatic figure of Gertrude Stein. Whether we think of Gertrude Stein as a sage, a mountebank, or an authentic poet, one fact has to be admitted: she has been a formidable phenomenon, influencing other writers more than one likes, perhaps, to realize. Nor can it be denied that the impact of her personality and "unintelligible" linguistic compositions tended to encourage a spirit of anti-intellectualism among her contemporaries. But this fact is paradoxical. Gertrude Stein was herself a keen student of philosophy; and although the voice that speaks in her work is often playful and sometimes, in spite of her wit, uncompromisingly ordinary, the structure of her underlying ideas reveals that she had thought deeply about man's essential humanity and about the nature of the cosmos in which this humanity is possible.

That Gertrude Stein had a deep and persistent interest in philosophy should not surprise us. She was at an early stage involved in the most fruitful currents of modern thought. As a Radcliffe College undergraduate, she came under the influence of two of Harvard's greatest teachers: George Santayana, for whose philosophy she developed a lifelong admiration, and William James, under whose guidance she became for a time a serious student of philosophy and psychology.[2] Thus she had plenty of opportunity even in her

2. Under the direction of Hugo Münsterberg, Gertrude Stein collaborated in experiments in fatigue which were published under the title "Normal Motor Automatism," by Leon Solomons and Gertrude Stein, in *Psychological Review*, September 1896. The first writing of her own ever printed was "Cultivated Motor Automatism: A Study of Character in Its Relation to Attention," *Psychological Review*, May 1898.

formative years to appreciate some of the growing points of philosophical creation. Later she not only became acquainted with the work of Bergson (at least she attended lectures by him), but became a warmly cordial friend and admirer of Alfred North Whitehead. And to the reader who takes pains to decipher the recurrent ideograms in *The Geographical History of America,* or who has focused upon such "difficult" compositions as *An Acquaintance with Description* and *How To Write,* it seems clear that she was exploring some of the problems of meaning brought to the fore by such different linguistic philosophers as I. A. Richards and Ludwig Wittgenstein.

It is also abundantly clear that not only was she familiar with the great philosophical systems of the past, but that her explicit repudiation of systematic philosophy (and dogmatic religion as well) stemmed not from any distaste for metaphysics but from a deep dissatisfaction with systems that did not adequately recognize, or account for, her own primary philosophical intuition. Even as a young woman in college she was no merely passive student. In one of her Radcliffe themes, she ridiculed the Herbartian metaphysical notion of a real but unknowable world of *Wesen,* which she described as a quantity of nameless nothings, without time, space, form, or relation, yet which can combine to give us our world of appearances.[3] She evidently found philosophy too rationalistic, for she wrote many years later, "When I was at college I studied philosophy that was it they did not know what they saw because they said they saw what they knew, and if they saw it they no longer knew it because then

3. Rosalind S. Miller, *Gertrude Stein: Form and Intelligibility* (New York: Exposition Press, 1949), p. 132.

they were two" (GHA, 150). Actually her interest in the fundamental problems of philosophy never left her, but she returned to them by way of art.

Viewed from the vantage point of occupied France in 1943-44, Gertrude Stein's life in retrospect appeared to her to have been a part of the dialectical movement of history in which a new generation realizes itself by detachment from the past and attachment to the future that is in the making: "I belong to the generation who born in the nineteenth century spent all the early part of my life escaping from it, and the rest of it in being the twentieth century yes of course" (WIHS, 80). Thus, after the fact, she saw her own instinctive creative drive as part of the movement that overthrew the utopianism and optimism so widespread at the turn of the century. She could even think of herself as a dragon killer, along with St. George and Siegfried—her dragon, the modern dragon, being the nineteenth-century belief in science and progress. During her childhood there had been no dragons except in fairy tales. Instead, there was evolution: "Evolution was all over my childhood, walks abroad with an evolutionist and the world was full of evolution, biological and botanical evolution, with music as a background for emotion and books as a reality, and a great deal of fresh air as a necessity, and a great deal of eating as an excitement and an orgy" (WIHS, 17).

Since the mental climate of the period discouraged excessive concern with the mysteries of life and death, Gertrude Stein suffered secretly and intensely from the fear of death. She refers more than once to the agony of her girlhood in California—to her melancholy, her "rather desperate inner life," and "the dark and dreadful days of adolescence." In a Radcliffe theme called "The Temptation" she seems to be writing autobiographically when she tells of a girl who attends an evening church service during which she reflects upon the significance of kneeling in prayer, while at the same time longing and questioning—yearning "to throw off the weight, the intolerable burden of solving for herself the great world-problems." [4]

During her years at Radcliffe and Johns Hopkins she certainly became more extroverted, but if we are to believe that in *The Making of Americans,* an autobiographical novel, she was writing of her own departure for Europe, it is clear that she had a strong sense of alienation:

Brother Singulars, we are misplaced in a generation that knows not Joseph. We flee before the disapproval of our cousins, the courageous condescension of our friends who gallantly sometimes agree to walk the streets with us, from all of them who never in any way can understand why such ways and not the others are dear to us, we fly to the kindly comfort of an older world accustomed to take all manner of strange forms into its bosom. (20)

Viewed from the outside, however, she became an expatriate more or less accidentally. Financially independent, subject to ennui, at loose ends—in London during the winter of 1902-3, she spent her days mostly in the British Museum, reading the Elizabethans. She had just turned her back upon scientific laboratories and hospital wards after failing to take a medical degree at Johns Hopkins, where she had gone (at James's suggestion) to prepare for the practice of pathological psychology. According to her own account of her

4. Miller, p. 154.

reading at the time, she was most diverted by the prose of
Robert Greene, but it is pleasant to imagine her also reading
Friar Bacon and Friar Bungay, that delightful comedy satir-
izing medieval pseudo-science. She may well have felt, what
with the menstruums, incantations, and "spirits" employed
by the two old necromancers, a similarity to the planchettes,
tuning forks, and pistols employed in the psychological experiments of her Radcliffe days, performed under the direction of James and Hugo Münsterberg. In particular, her own
experiments and those of her fellow students Leon Solomons
and Boris Sidis, in automatic writing and other unconscious
reactions, had been no more fruitful in laying open the mysteries of the human mind than had the abortive labors of
Friar Bacon, whose fabricated "monstrous head of brass"
could say nothing more revealing of the mysteries of the
universe than "Time is . . . Time was . . . Time is past."

In the spring of 1903 she joined her brother Leo in Paris
and began her long, spectacular career as an American expatriate and a member of the avant-garde. Soon engrossed
in the purchase of modern paintings, beginning with a
Cézanne, for nearly fifty years she continued to evince a
lively interest in the work of such abstractionists as Picasso,
Picabia, Braque, and Juan Gris. At some early moment
(*Q.E.D.,* her first novel, is dated 1903) she began to write,
and in the course of the years became associated with an
international group of writers and painters dedicated to the
pursuit of novel methods of expression. Conspicuous among
its members were the cubists, who looked mainly to Guillaume Apollinaire to rationalize their goals, but who derived
their earliest inspiration from the work of Picasso.

In *Picasso* (1938), Gertrude Stein said that she was naturally "with" cubism from the first because she was doing the

same kind of thing in her writing, and she gave three reasons for the emergence of the cubistic vision:

First. The composition, because the way of living had changed the composition of living had extended and each thing was as important as any other thing. Secondly, the faith in what the eyes were seeing, that is to say the belief in the reality of science, commenced to diminish . . .

Thirdly, the framing of life, the need that a picture exist in its frame, remain in its frame was over. (12)

Indeed, for anyone sensitive to the modern time-spirit, the universe seemed a great deal less rational, less unified, less stable, less concrete than it had once appeared. In Gertrude Stein's words, "The twentieth century has much less reasonableness in its existence than the nineteenth century but reasonableness does not make for splendor . . . It is a time when everything cracks, where everything is destroyed, everything isolates itself, it is a more splendid thing than a period where everything follows itself" (P, 49).

In the course of the decade before the First World War, Gertrude Stein participated in the furor and excitement of a revolutionary movement in the arts, which seemed bent upon the destruction of authority and the established order everywhere, in behalf of a "new vision." After the war, her role was catalytic, accelerating the processes of change among the members of the younger generation of American writers who visited the Rue de Fleurus. For forty years she worked at her writing, gradually getting it published and ultimately becoming an international figure of almost legendary proportions. When she died in 1946 her literary remains had already been deposited in the library of one of America's great universities, and its press became committed to their publication in a series of eight volumes, now completed, called the Yale Edition of the Unpublished Writings of Gertrude Stein.

Nonetheless, the deliberate hermeticism of much of Stein's work has made her aesthetic theories and practices suspect. The writings often resemble alchemical projections both in the operations that produced them and in the end for which they were produced. Her goal appears to be something almost quintessential—the mastery perhaps of a power like that attributed to the seekers after the philosopher's stone or to Thoth, the legendary Egyptian deity of wisdom and magic, measurer of time and inventor of numbers, to whom were anciently ascribed the beginnings of civilization. Thus to the world she has appeared, at worst, as a conjurer exercising the arts of trickery and deception and, at best, as a kind of Magus in pursuit of some magical incantation that would release, not genius, but a jinni. The equivocal nature of both the goal and the "projections" arouses justifiable suspicion, for its methods seem ineffectual, involving the use of magic formulas and "universal solvents" that resolve or dissolve nothing. Consequently, over the years many a glancing blow has been struck at her "soporific rigmaroles and echolaliac incantations." [5] But it was Wyndham Lewis in *Time and Western Man* (1927) who launched the first major attack against the aesthetic assumptions not only of Gertrude Stein but of the "time-philosophers" (chiefly Bergson, Alexander, and Whitehead) and their disciples in the arts.

Using Stein as a whipping boy in four chapters entitled "Tests for Counterfeit in the Arts," "A Brief Account of the Child-Cult," "Time-Children: Miss Gertrude Stein and Miss

5. Edmund Wilson, *Axel's Castle* (New York: Charles Scribner's Sons, 1931), p. 253.

Anita Loos," and "The Prose-Song of Gertrude Stein," Lewis wittily stigmatized her as a denizen of "highly-intellectualized High-Bohemia," "a jazz sibyl," "a faux-naïf," "an Epstein in words," and "a Monument sitting upon patience." Without denying the viability of the time-philosophy as a system of abstract truth, he waged open war upon all practitioners of the arts who revealed "an exasperated time-sense" and, identifying vision *sub specie aeternitatis* with the Bergsonian *durée*, relativized all values and made an absolute of their own "exclusive and peculiar sensibilities." The "monstrous, desperate, soggy lengths of primitive mass-life" of *Three Lives* appeared to him "undoubtedly intended as an epic contribution to the present mass-democracy" and, as such, examples of "the false 'revolutionary,' propagandist *plainmanism* of her time." Listing three main objections to her work—its deadness, its decadent romanticism, its unreality— he compared it to Picasso's painting and classified both artists as "nature-mortists." [6]

Today Lewis' assault upon the aesthetic principles of a whole school of artists which included Joyce, Proust, Picasso, and Gertrude Stein seems all too familiar. But his foray against Stein, though only a flanking action in his general attack, was particularly devastating because it impugned her integrity. Granting her "force" and "robust intelligence," he saw in her naiveté a masquerade, pseudo-intellectual, snobbish, and decadent, assumed to cover up a fundamental capitulation of reason to primitivism and irrationality. He deplored the effort on the part of stream-of-consciousness writers to introspect their own creative processes, though he did not deny the mystery of creativity: "A great artist falls

6. Wyndham Lewis, *Time and Western Man* (London: Chatto and Windus, 1927), pp. 65-81.

into a trance of sorts when he creates," he said, "about that there is little doubt." [7] But any effort to express the stream of consciousness in itself is fruitless: it is only "unorganized word-dreaming of the mind when not concentrated for some logical functioning purpose." Further, "The mind demands some special substance from a writer, for words open into the region of ideas; and the requirements of that region, where it is words you are using, must somehow be met." [8] Separated from some naturalistic framework, the stream-of-consciousness technique results, in Lewis' words, in "picturesque dementia"—a fabric of airy nothings, though not without a local habitation and even a name. Their local habitation is, however, the interior of a mind whose confines are closed even to the "I" defining its boundaries. Forced to move about in compositions purporting to reveal the mind's landscape, Lewis suffered, as many others have done, from claustrophobia and was inclined to call the author a sham.

One of Lewis' chief objections to the time-philosophers and their disciples in the arts was their tendency to associate creative work with prayer. His acute distress before any such equation comes out in his chapter "Pure Poetry and Pure Magic." Though he spoke of the artist as a dreamer and of creative writing as "a spell, a talisman, an incantation," very likely the manipulation of a supernatural power, for him literature did not play the role of "sacred books" as it did in antiquity: "For me art is the civilized *substitute* for magic; as philosophy is what, on a higher or more complex plane, takes the place of religion." Thus he aimed a shaft at Henri Brémond, one of the authors of *La Poésie pure*. Brémond had countered Pater's assertion that "all art seeks to approx-

7. *Ibid.*, p. 129.
8. *Ibid.*, pp. 121, 123.

imate to that of music" with an even more equivocal assertion, which Lewis translated: "No, they [the arts] all of them
aspire each one by means of its own appropriate magic—
words, notes, colours, lines—all aspire to become a *prayer.*"
To this Lewis responded, "Brémond is a religionist masquer-
ading as an artist or critic of art, or a philosopher." [9]

But the dreamlike state of creativity has made artists from
time immemorial feel both religious and philosophical, and
many a modern poet has sought to describe the creative
state. Of one such description, E. M. Forster has this to say:

The French writer, Paul Claudel, gives the best description
known to me of the creative state. It occurs in *La Ville.* A poet
is speaking. He has been asked whence his inspiration comes,
and how is it when he speaks everything becomes applicable
although he explains nothing. He replies:

I do not speak what I wish, but I conceive in sleep,
And I cannot explain whence I draw my breath, for it is my
          breath which is drawn out of me.
I expand the emptiness within me, I open my mouth, I
          breathe in the air, I breathe it out.
I restore it in the form of an intelligible word,
And having spoken I know what I have said.[10]

Further to emphasize the disparity between self-conscious
and unself-conscious mental operations, Forster adds, "Think
before you speak is criticism's motto; speak before you think
creation's." This witty antithesis obviously is only another
way of expressing the sheer spontaneity of creativity.

One of the primary purposes of the time-philosophers has

---

9. *Ibid.*, pp. 188-199. *La Poésie pure* (Paris: Bernard Grasset, 1926) contains a series of discourses by Henri Brémond and Robert Souza.
10. "What I Believe," *Two Cheers for Democracy* (New York: Harcourt,
Brace and World, 1951), p. 115.

been to account for emergent novelty in the arts and to construct an aesthetics consonant with the findings of the biological sciences and of psychology. They have therefore emphasized indeterminism in nature itself; and they have written of creativity as a manifestation of an *élan vital,* a life force, a dynamism, inhering in an organism that develops in time—an energy irradiating the whole of nature, endlessly dividing and synthesizing. Bergson, who ended in mysticism, said, "The universe is a machine for the making of gods." [11] Whitehead, who was a mathematician before he was a philosopher and to whom Gertrude Stein was intellectually closer than to Bergson, avoided mysticism by assuming an essential reciprocal reference between mental and physical "occasions": "For things to be together involves that they are rationally together." His philosophy of organism, like Bergson's, included the element of time in creativity: "In the most literal sense the lapse of time is the renovation of the world of ideas." For him, "all aesthetic experience is feeling arising out of the realization of contrast under identity." Going beyond the truth of religious creeds, he said, "The religious insight is the grasp of this truth . . . that the universe exhibits a creativity with infinite freedom, and a realm of forms with infinite possibilities; but that this creativity and these forms are together impotent to achieve actuality apart from that completed ideal harmony, which is God." [12]

Whitehead's conception of the religious nature of expression seems especially relevant to Gertrude Stein's attitude toward writing. "Expression," he said, "is the one fundamental sacrament. It is the outward and visible sign of an

11. *The Two Sources of Morality and Religion* (New York: Henry Holt and Company, 1935), p. 306.
12. *Religion in the Making* (New York: Macmillan Company, 1926), pp. 115, 119.

inward and spiritual grace." Firsthand expression, or creation, is extremely rare—the work of a few geniuses, whose
"peculiar originality is the very element in their expression
which remains unformularized. They deal with what all men
know, and they make it new. They do not bring into the
world a new formula nor do they discover new facts, but
in expressing their apprehension of the world, they leave
behind them an element of novelty—a new expression forever
evoking its proper response." [13]

William James's conceptions of saintliness and vocation
resemble rather closely Whitehead's sacramental view of
expression. James denied the existence of any such entity as
religious emotion. He defined religion as "the feelings, acts,
and experiences of individual men in their solitude, so far
as they apprehend themselves to stand in relation to whatever they may consider divine." The divine, however, need
not be personified. For him "divine" meant "God-*like*, whether it be a concrete deity or not." [14] He disliked the term
"transcendental Ego," but he was willing on speculative
grounds to regard it as a substitute for the "thinking I"; his
pragmatic acceptance of religious faith lies at the very heart
of his teachings, though as a philosopher he rejected all
absolutes and subscribed to a pluralistic universe.

James distinguished between saints and hysterics in terms
of their expression—their works. As far as he was concerned,
there are many ways of being saintly: for example, being
"true to one's mission and vocation." He differentiated between ordinary people and geniuses solely in terms of "the
amount of steam-pressure chronically driving the character

13. *Ibid.*, pp. 131, 135-136.
14. *The Varieties of Religious Experience* (New York: Modern Library,
1936) [Longmans, Green and Company, 1902]), pp. 31-32, 34.

in an ideal direction, or the amount of ideal excitement tran-
siently acquired." [15] He was convinced that "There is a
continuum of cosmic consciousness, against which our individuality builds accidental fences, and into which our several
minds plunge as into a mother-sea or reservoir." [16] In the
prayer state he found the condition that brings about an
influx of cosmic energy: prayer consists basically of holding
open "the subliminal door" of consciousness in a subjective
state of receptivity.

Perhaps Charles Sanders Peirce has characterized this kind
of consciousness better than any of the other philosophers
who have linked creativity with religion on pragmatic
grounds. He called it "musement," which according to one
of his interpreters meant

an occupation of the mind which "involves no purpose save that
of casting aside all serious purpose," and which consists in wonder . . . The attitude of mind involved is close to *pure play* because it is not fraught with serious purpose of any kind; on the
contrary, it is actually an attempt to cut through the layers of
conscious purpose and arrive at that state of mind which is close
to the naïveté and freshness of children in the face of some awe-
inspiring wonder. If, however, some ulterior purpose is allowed
to enter, the proper attitude is destroyed.[17]

Gertrude Stein displays in her writing precisely the sacramental view of human creativity to which Forster subscribed, to which Lewis so strenuously objected, and which
is central to the thought of Peirce, James, Bergson, and

15. *Ibid.*, p. 261.
16. Quoted by Lloyd Morris in *William James* (New York: Charles Scribner's Sons, 1950), p. 64.
17. John E. Smith, "Religion and Theology," *Studies in the Philosophy
of Peirce*, ed. Philip P. Wiener and Frederic H. Young (Cambridge: Harvard University Press, 1952), pp. 260-261.

Whitehead. Like William James in particular, she was always interested in the psychology of religion (witness the numerous passages in *The Making of Americans*), but her correlation of creativity and prayer seems to be very different from a merely scientific or literary interest. This correlation did not reveal itself explicitly in her work until after 1908, and then only in murmured words. About 1920, however, beginning with "A Hymn," it appeared often in her titles, notably "Saints and Singing: A Play," "A Saint in Seven," "Lend a Hand: Four Religions," and "Talks to Saints, or Stories of Saint Remy"—all dated 1922. It was also in 1922 that she wrote to Kate Buss to the effect that there was no threshold between her conscious and her unconscious mind,[18] a detail of some significance since in 1923 she wrote "An Elucidation," her first effort at explaining her work. In it appeared the following passage:

To begin elucidating.
If I say I stand and pray.
If I say I stand and I stand and you understand and if I say I pray I pray to-day if you understand me to say I pray to-day you understand prayers and portraits.[19]

Here the tone is that of one who has abandoned mechanistic theories of creative expression, who is "acting on faith." Taken with her earlier assertion that she knew no threshold between the conscious and the unconscious, and with her increasing choice of saints as the ostensible subjects of her

18. See *The Flowers of Friendship*, ed. Donald Gallup (New York: Alfred A. Knopf, 1953), p. 150. Kate Buss wrote, "I should like to know how you know there is no demarcation between your thinking and your unthinking mind. I don't see how you CAN know that."
19. "An Elucidation," *Transition*, supplement (April 1927), p. 4. The date of composition is given in *A Catalogue of the Published and Unpublished Writings of Gertrude Stein*, comp. Robert Bartlett Haas and Donald Clifford Gallup (New Haven: Yale University Library, 1941).

compositions, "If I say I stand and pray" suggests the kind of decision that, according to James in *The Will To Believe,* transforms velleities into realizations. In other words, Gertrude Stein was saying that she was daily putting herself in a "faith state" or "prayer state"—opening her mind upon its inner domain.

Her interest in the faith state of religious votaries apparently reached its peak in 1927 in the opera *Four Saints in Three Acts* and the prose work *Lucy Church Amiably.* But in 1932 came the "Grant" section of *Four in America,* a meditation on American religion, and in 1938 she composed another opera, *Doctor Faustus Lights the Lights,* which has theological implications. Thus her concern with prayer and saints, so reminiscent of James's *Varieties of Religious Experience,* is central to her work. In fact, her correlation of writing and prayer implies more than a poet's exaltation or a psychologist's interest in the creative process. Yet whatever her goal was, or whatever the nature of the breakthrough referred to in the letter to Kate Buss, it apparently had nothing to do with leading a saintly life or with the transports of the mystic. I suggest that both her goal and the breakthrough were aesthetic and philosophical in essence.

In "Another Garland for Gertrude Stein," the foreword to *What Are Masterpieces,* Robert Bartlett Haas suggests that Gertrude Stein went "beyond James to develop an indigenous American aesthetics," and he speaks of her as having for over thirty years "struggled to give our literature the backbone of a native metaphysic." In his introduction to *The Geographical History of America,* Thornton Wilder refers to her as a "creative metaphysician." Some of her more recent critics and biographers, with varying degrees of sympathy or antipathy, have attempted to account for the idiosyncrasies of her work in terms of a highly individual philosophical theory. For the most part, however, the emphasis has been upon the links between her compositional techniques and those of the cubist painters rather than upon the similarities between her underlying philosophical views and those of modern philosophers. Michael J. Hoffman, in his recent valuable study, notes her connections with "almost all the intellectual and artistic movements of the time." [20] Donald Sutherland, one of her most sympathetic interpreters, emphasizes the importance for her of the Jamesian conception of consciousness as a "relation or a function," of the thinker as the "passing thought." Of her philosophy he says, "The idea that the present thing is the final reality was to be the axis or pole of Gertrude Stein's universe, and her work from the beginning was oriented and reoriented upon this idea." [21] Grounding his defense of her writings on the freedom of the individual, Sutherland finds her verbal constructions "an expression of as serious a philosophical position and as valid and heroic a way of life as any, which is that man can and must constantly and, in the last analysis, arbitrarily, choose for himself and be on his own . . . The philosophy is radically one of freedom within a fairly strict empiricism." [22]

More recently, in correspondence, Sutherland has written that among Gertrude Stein's early influences two philosophers might be cardinal: Spinoza and Santayana. But though it may be a short step, as Sutherland has suggested, from "All things are in God" to "Anything is something," there

20. *The Development of Abstractionism in the Writings of Gertrude Stein* (Philadelphia: University of Pennsylvania Press, 1965), p. 84.
21. *Gertrude Stein: A Biography of Her Work* (New Haven: Yale University Press, 1951), pp. 6-7.
22. *Ibid.*, p. 84.

seems to me no indication, in a philosophy that is one of freedom and empiricism, that Stein owed any debt to Spinoza's logical pantheism. As for the other, not only was Gertrude Stein a student of Santayana's at Radcliffe, but even a fairly superficial comparison opens up a set of interesting correspondences between the two (although whether or not they took the same attitude toward freedom must remain debatable). Like Santayana, to begin with, Gertrude Stein creates a philosophy that is naturalistic and indeed unflinchingly materialistic, with no reliance on any sense of cosmic purpose and no softening of the antithesis between nature on the one hand and spirit, or "the human mind," on the other. Like Santayana, too, she treats with total lack of belief, yet with the utmost tenderness, the symbols of traditional Catholic faith: saints and sanctity, ritual and prayer. Finally, in spite of this basically naturalistic viewpoint, she has, like Santayana, made certain concessions to Platonism and Platonic doctrines of being and essence. And like him she regards aesthetic creation, religion, and philosophy as belonging to the same spiritual sphere.

Heroic individualism is probably the key to the resemblance here. John Malcolm Brinnin also speaks with sympathy of the heroic quality of her effort, although in his opinion it is mainly inspired not by philosophy, but by the cubistic vision. Even cubism, however, had its philosophical foundation.[23] Brinnin nonetheless sees in her compositions

23. According to George Lemaitre, *From Cubism to Surrealism in French Literature* (Cambridge: Harvard University Press, 1941), Guillaume Apollinaire, the chief formulator of cubist philosophy, "explained not only to the public but even to the painters themselves the goal toward which they were almost unconsciously tending" (p. 100). This philosophy reflected an aspiration "to penetrate beneath the motley exterior of material appearances and to grasp something of the fundamental substance of reality" (pp. 79-80). Partly mystical, cubism had in it an intellectual element: "Strangely

merely the stringent application to language of cubistic techniques of analysis, collage, and nonrepresentational construction. In his opinion, her efforts were directed toward the exploration of the plastic potentialities of language. Though he notes her "lifelong philosophical relationship" with William James and says parenthetically that she was never a disciple of Bergson's, Brinnin feels that the philosophical basis of her aesthetic theories and practices is unimportant and that, in any case, the traces of James's (or anyone else's) influence have been largely effaced by her preoccupation with cubistic techniques:

Her writing was loosely based in what she had learned from William James, and its sources can be traced back to certain of her experiments and pronouncements on the nature of consciousness. But the connection with James is neither strong enough nor consistent enough to base a theory upon. Except for those affinities that might be explained as merely coincidental, she herself quite naturally denied the relationship between the "vision" of her works and the laboratory documentations of her old master. Her deepest and most immediate sources lay in paint-

---

enough, their mysticism was blended with a thoroughly mathematical conception of the world . . . Even though discursive logic was discredited, the Cubists had little difficulty in persuading themselves that pure geometry reflected the basic architecture of the universe . . . Soon they were convinced that by systematic computation and clever combination of circles and angles, they would be able to attain the truer reality for which they were longing" (p. 80). Inspired by Baudelaire and Rimbaud as well as by Negro art, "the Cubists set out to dislocate the world of appearances, combining the dissociated elements according to a new order. This had the advantages—now implicitly recognized—of breaking up banal associations that rob every aspect of reality of its individual force and disclosing a view of the transcendental that each of them may hold. This new order was not to be determined logically, nor even mathematically, but solely by intuition" (p. 81). In the course of its development, cubism broke up into several kinds, classified by Lemaitre as scientific, orphic, physical, and instinctive. Picasso always remained a scientific cubist in his purpose of making "the precise investigation of a fundamental reality" (p. 90).

ing; and by the time she had transcribed the lessons of painting into her own practice, connections that might possibly have indicated her dependence on any but her own existential "frame of reference" were severed.[24]

On the other hand, her severest recent critic, B. L. Reid, emphasizes the affinity between her theories and methods and those of modern philosophers: "The important thing to note is that somehow she had made her way into the main stream of contemporary philosophy, and probably art as well, in her preoccupation with time and with thought process as reality." Denying the viability of her philosophy, Reid hazards a guess concerning the method by which she sought to achieve her goal of "the exact reproduction of an inner or outer reality," suggesting she might have been influenced by the phenomenologists: "What we have here is something very close to the so-called 'reduction' process of the Phenomenologists, and one cannot help wondering whether Miss Stein had not encountered Husserl or his followers." [25]

He thinks it more likely, however, that she had merely taken too narrowly and too literally James's injunction to "keep your mind open." Acknowledging that in her critical-aesthetic writings "she is wholly serious and genuinely, but not always deeply or originally, philosophical" and that "her system is perfectly coherent," he is inclined to excuse what he regards as her literary misbehavior on the ground that she was a victim of pathological self-alienation, of "cultivated schizophrenia." [26]

24. John Malcolm Brinnin, *The Third Rose: Gertrude Stein and Her World* (Boston and Toronto: Little, Brown and Company, 1959), p. 301.
25. B. L. Reid, *Art by Subtraction: A Dissenting Opinion of Gertrude Stein* (Norman: University of Oklahoma Press, 1958), pp. 47, 66.
26. *Ibid.*, pp. 202-203.

The continental philosopher F. H. Heinemann has expressed a somewhat similar judgment of Gertrude Stein in *Existentialism and the Modern Predicament,* in which he cites her (along with Schönberg and Picasso) as an example of "technological alienation"—a widespread phenomenon apparent among modern intellectuals attributable partly to "the progressive mechanization of life." In one passage where he is bringing out the prevalent emphasis upon method in science, the arts, and philosophy, he links Stein's name to those of the linguistic philosophers, noting a similarity between the Steinian colloquial style and that of John Wisdom, a follower of Wittgenstein's. As another major factor contributing to alienation, Heinemann calls attention to the importance of Hegel's philosophy, referring particularly to such topics as "Spirit in Self-Estrangement: Culture" and "Language as the Actuality of Alienation or of Culture" discussed by Hegel in *The Phenomenology of Mind.* He finds Hegel's view of language of topical interest, for "If Hegel is right, if Language represents a specific mode of self-estrangement, then we have to ask ourselves whether the preoccupation with language as language in our time, is not an expression of the very estrangement which we are discussing." [27]

Heinemann's casual collocation of Stein and Wittgenstein may be more important than the pun involved in their names, and the relevance he finds in Hegel's description of language as cultural alienation bears directly upon Steinian thought. Though Alice B. Toklas has said that Gertrude Stein did not know Wittgenstein, [28] there do seem to be significant verbal

27. F. H. Heinemann, *Existentialism and the Modern Predicament* (New York: Harper and Brothers, 1958), pp. 10-11.
28. In answer to my inquiry regarding Gertrude Stein's indebtedness to various philosophers, Miss Toklas wrote: "Gertrude Stein didn't know

echoes of Wittgenstein's *Tractatus Logico-Philosophicus* (published in England, 1922) in Stein's "An Elucidation" (1927), written in 1923, and in the pieces comprising *How To Write* (1931), composed after 1926. Moreover, her play with words may be called "language games," and her hermetic writing may be regarded as an effort to "make a new move" in the usage of the English language. Indeed, it is quite possible to associate her ideas with Hegel's theories of language and culture in *The Phenomenology of Mind*.

A close reading of Stein has persuaded me that she was very likely familiar with this work. In any case, the movement of thought in much of her writing seems to parallel the dialectical movement of the Hegelian world spirit in a moment of transition and transformation, namely, the twentieth century. In fact, each of the three compositions I concentrate on in the following chapters records some aspect of the process of transformation. *Tender Buttons* embodies the appearance of the new as bare abstraction in an isolated mind. *The Geographical History of America, or The Relation of Human Nature to the Human Mind* is a meditation on the general spiritual impoverishment and abstractness of American consciousness. *Doctor Faustus Lights the Lights* dramatizes the psychic process of alienation from nature and the salutary transformation of the archetypal images of the Western Mind into the concrete actuality of experience. According to my view, Gertrude Stein was always recording, not experiences, but the "experiencings," of the Hegelian world spirit as an internal drama on the simultaneous

---

Wittgenstein. She was a pupil of Santayana and towards the end of his life we went down to Rome to visit him, but he was no longer there . . . She was under the influence of James and Whitehead of course, but not Bergson."

stage of her own consciousness and of Western man's—a drama in which the actors are words, those relatively stable objects of the human mind in a changing world.

If I am right in classifying Stein's work as a phenomonology of mind, then theoretically I ought to concentrate on the correlation between her thought and Hegel's. But, in a practical sense, such a comparison would be too restrictive on the one hand and too broad on the other. For one thing, most English and American philosophers at the turn of the century set out mainly from Hegel; thus the outline of the Hegelian dialectical process is perceptible in much of their thought. Furthermore, it is really more to the point to relate Stein's ideas to those of her contemporaries, conspicuously, but not exclusively, James, Bergson, and Whitehead, whose distinctive views were developed during her own "continuous present." In the second place, the Hegelian dialectic is such a completely formulated system, and so comprehensive, that in spite of Hegel's determinism the transformations he envisions resemble those postulated by biological evolution, which played an important part in the work of the process-philosophers and even in Jung's account of the process of individuation. Similarly, in the context of universal history, the Hegelian dialectical movement recalls Vico's account of the growth of civilization—or Eli Faure's Spirit of the Forms. In truth, wherever processes of change in man and society are described, the gestalt is much the same. Take Bergson, for example: his evolutionary theory of creativity, his belief that "the universe is a machine for the making of gods," his *élan vital*, may appear to be the antithesis of Hegelian thought; yet in their descriptions of the emergence of the new, Bergson and Hegel have much in common. All in all, it seems more fruitful to survey the field in seeking for the sources of Gertrude Stein's weltan-schauung than to limit research to the work of any one philosopher.

Again, and most important, I am interested primarily in Gertrude Stein and her writing as a manifestation of the twentieth-century spirit—in the image projected by her and through her of Western man's alienation from nature and from his past. Though I want to set her thought against the background of perennial philosophy, I want also to examine it as a phenomenon of her era. This leads me to vary my approach to the various works. Thus my chapter "Language and Vision" discusses her metaphysical assumptions and their implications insofar as these can be deduced from *The Geographical History*. The purpose of "Selfhood and the Word" is to perform the act of penetrating beneath the flat surface of the vocabulary in *Tender Buttons,* the most signi-ficant of her hermetic compositions. "An American Version of the Faust Legend" interprets in Jungian terms the modern psyche as Gertrude Stein projects it in *Doctor Faustus Lights the Lights.*

Just as there is a difference in approach in each chapter, inevitably there is some repetition throughout. As Gertrude Stein often put it, everything is always the same and always different. Because, as she said in *An Acquaintance with Des-cription,* she had resolved to "describe it where it is at its widest," her philosophical ideas are everywhere interrelated and recurrent. When there is so much radiation, the process of tracing a single strand is very like unraveling a piece of knitting (whether hand-made or machine-made): in spite

of the many discrete loops by which the garment is constructed, there is really only one thread. Wishing to demonstrate
the free play of the human mind in the structures of its
knowing at any time, she always recapitulates what has been
woven on the loom of history as she weaves the garment of
her own thought.

One more word remains to be added here. When Gertrude
Stein was writing, she was also pointing to language itself,
something present to everyone, but indefinable—something
unnamed and unnamable, pervading every man's knowledge
of himself and his world. Language mirrors, in its stable
"names" and grammatical structures, everything that can
be thought of; but, as Wittgenstein puts it, "that which mirrors itself in language language cannot represent." [29] Speaking in the broadest context of all our symbolic forms, Ernst
Cassirer says the same thing in another way: "The question
as to what myth, religion, art, language 'are' cannot be answered in a purely abstract way, by a logical definition . . .
or solved by merely historical investigations." [30] From still
another point of view, Karl Jaspers, the "floating philosopher," characterizes authentic being as "shapeless." [31] And
the phenomenologist Husserl, by his method of eidetic reduction, is said to have believed he had discovered a phenomenal residuum—a "nonpsychological I" or "anonymous
consciousness that does not belong to anybody." [32] In its
way, Gertrude Stein's writing after 1908 may be taken as a
gesture in the direction of all of these ideas.

29. Ludwig Wittgenstein, *Tractatus Logico-Philosophicus* (New York:
Harcourt, Brace and Company, 1922), proposition 4.1212.
30. Ernst Cassirer, *An Essay on Man* (New York: Doubleday and Company, 1953), p. 154.
31. Heinemann, p. 62.
32. *Ibid.*, p. 53.

The Tao that can be told of
Is not the Absolute Tao;
The Names that can be given
Are not Absolute Names.

The Nameless is the origin of Heaven and
Earth;
The Named is the Mother of all Things.
        —Laotse (translation by Lin Yutang)

II. LANGUAGE AND VISION:
A CLUE TO STEINIAN THOUGHT

As I observed in the opening chapter, Gertrude Stein's explicit repudiation of systematic philosophy and dogmatic religion did not stem from any aversion to the use of reason. Quite the contrary. But she did have a genuine philosophical insight of her own—a singularly clear perception of certain aspects of experience and of cosmic reality to which, she seems to have felt, most philosophical systems failed to do justice. Needless to say, she did not expound her own philosophy in any systematic way. Yet it is possible to gather from her work that she was always concerned with "the moment [that] is not a moment"—an act, although it "does nothing"—and one that is effective in the creation of "masterpieces." And from *The Geographical History of America* in particular one can get a fairly clear idea of what this primary philosophical intuition of hers really amounts to, and how it is related to her literary work and creative purpose.

The first thing that strikes the reader of her work as a whole is that the emotion contained in it is a genuine cosmic emotion (almost religious, according to James's definition of religion), but focused less upon first and last things than upon the potentialities and latencies of experience. Her metaphysical thinking is thus naturally concerned with the mystery of creativity—with the primal source of emergent novelty in the world and of creative insight in man. For although she was a thoroughgoing temporalist and pluralist, in the best Jamesian tradition, Stein recognized, like James himself, the miraculous element in the advent of the *new;* and in her life and work it was always the new that she cared about most. Her theory of the possible discontinuity between being and existence is an effort to describe this miracle.

Even more significant, perhaps, is the quality of her reflection upon the nature of being. A modern temporalist might deny that this word "being" (except with reference to the subsistent forms of mathematics and logic) means anything different from "existence." But for Gertrude Stein there was a difference; and since she was an empiricist it was a difference that could be seen only after being and existence had been united, in experience. Her name for this increment of depth in existence is "being existing," a predicative term that recurs throughout her writing and that emphasizes the interplay of self-activity (an individual's entelechy) and his life history (his "existing"). Ultimately this locution seems to express fullness of being, clarity of perception, and detachment from egocentric claims. It becomes practically synonymous, indeed, with her conception of the "human mind." Here again her theory of the moment of discontinuity between being and existence is crucial. For at any level "being existing" unites past and future—but at its highest level it is the product of this moment, not of causal forces.

Gertrude Stein lived and did her work in accordance with these great ideas. Perhaps to understand them is to understand both her extraordinary personal influence, about which all her critics and interpreters have something to say, and also the extraordinary vitality of her best writing, whether it is intelligible or not. At least we shall find that, in spite of the defects, failures, and occasional frivolity of her work, she was genuinely trying to bring the philosopher, in herself, closer to the poet. Her best work attempts to recreate "that unity which thought, as such, and poetry, as such, had in their beginnings."

Much of Gertrude Stein's philosophical thinking is expressed fully and maturely in *The Geographical History of America, or The Relation of Human Nature to the Human Mind,* published in 1936, only ten years before her death. As far as her fundamental ideas are concerned, then, the following discussion is based primarily on this difficult—but in its own way thoroughly charming—book, and especially on those aspects of it suggested in the alternative title, the relation of human nature to the human mind.

It is clear that Gertrude Stein, the favorite pupil of James and the friend of Whitehead, was very naturally concerned with the nature of freedom and the restrictions imposed on freedom by the causal relations of things in time. Certainly her "portraits" and "plays," as well as her various efforts to elucidate her work, reveal that she was seeking to break through language habits and literary patterns to affirm the openness of the universe against all determinisms.

This openness, which for most thinkers implies an element of radical discontinuity in the world, is entirely consistent with her basic assumption that there is no immortality for human personality. As a child she had been surprised to learn that "in the Old Testament there was nothing about a future life or eternity" (EA, 114). Later a knowledge of astronomy confirmed, for her, the finality of individual death; and there is no more dramatic instance of discontinuity, within human experience, than the brute finality of death. From the beginning of her intellectual life, moreover, she seems to have followed William James (who in this respect followed Renouvier) in a deeply felt acceptance of *novelty* as a genuine element in the cosmos. And to believe in real novelty is to believe not only in the reality of time;

it is also to believe in absolute beginnings, dissolutions, and discontinuities. Nevertheless, from her youth on, she had also been haunted by thoughts of identity, memory, and the bewildering concept of "eternity," with which identity and memory seem somehow to be involved. She resolved her difficulty (as many other thinkers have done) by a belief in the everlastingness and indestructibility of the cosmos in time. Time itself, she assumed, is of infinite duration—endless and immeasurable.[1]

This assumption that the cosmic process has an infinite past and an infinite future carries definite ontological and cosmological implications. For an antideterminist, however, it creates a puzzling difficulty. If we think of the modes of being, we are first confronted with the existential present actuality of experience, both mental and physical. But questions immediately arise as to the past (origins) and the future (destiny). What of the beginning and the end? There must be the possibility of being for anything to have become actual; but if time has no beginning, the possibility of being

1. The orthodox view of science presupposes an infinite past actuality, in spite of the unwilling conclusion of contemporary physicists that the present universe (as an "epoch," at least) must have had an abrupt beginning. Unlike philosophy (which may speak of God), science is required to continue in its search for causes. Possibility, for science and for many schools of philosophy, is meaningless without existence; but science must assume—as philosophy need not—that this existence is that of the cosmos, not of a Creator. Gertrude Stein everywhere implies, and especially in *The Geographical History*, that she accepts this scientific view. Again and again she derides, by implication, the idea that anything has a beginning, a middle, and an end; and from a consistently empirical standpoint she seems to deduce from what is open to inspection (as of course the past and future are not) that the universe itself has no beginning, no middle, and no end. Here is an especially clear statement of the view (GHA, 157-159): "Philosophy tells why nothing is begun but if it is not begun then there is no why. Inside anybody inside anybody inside knows there is no why to not begin because there is no such thing. No such thing as begin."

must always have resided in some actuality. Now actuality involves determinations; and an infinite past actuality seems to imply that destiny is fated, and that all that happens must happen as a consequence of an infinity of prior determinations. Ontologically, Gertrude Stein attempted to escape from this dilemma by positing a dualism of being and existence. Her cosmology, as we shall see, assumes that *chance* is an ultimate category of the existential universe.[2]

It is difficult to separate being and existence without recourse to Platonism, in some sense or other; but Gertrude Stein was not a Platonist in the traditional sense. In her view, "being" and "existing" are always (as for Platonists) a pair; but they are very closely wedded, even though each one of the married pair retains status as a separate member of the union. She concedes to Platonism, it would seem, that the modes of being differ from the modes of existence. But she did not like the static implications of the infinitive "to be" when it is followed by a complement. Both "being" and "existing," grammatically considered, are verbals: they express the dynamic idea of going on. For Gertrude Stein, therefore, *to be* anything meant *to exist*, in a certain way, in relation to time and identity; and she seems to have avoid-

---

2. Stein's cosmology is like that of Peirce in every important respect save as to an infinite past actuality versus an absolute beginning in time, or rather of the *cosmic process in time*. But this is a crucial point, metaphysically. Peirce believed that if chance is a genuine existential category, it follows that time—or at least the cosmic process in time—*must* have had an absolute beginning. (In this view, time and cosmic change may be regarded as mutually involving each other.) Gertrude Stein seems not to have felt the force of this argument, which can only be hinted at here. Peirce, of course, speaks frequently of an absolute beginning of the cosmos, and almost never of a beginning of time; but since he posits an original nullity, an absolute zero, this amounts to a beginning of time, in any sense in which time can be distinguished from eternity.

ed the purely Platonic notion of eternal Being divorced from actuality. This attitude toward Platonism (coupled with an honest concession to the perennial truth of Platonism) appears in the following passage:

> Become Because
> Beware of be.
> Be is not what no one can be what no one can see and certainly not what no one can say.
> Anybody can say be.
> Be is for biography.
> And for autobiography.
> No not for autobiography because be comes after.
> So once more to renounce because and become.[3] (GHA, 156)

Here the alpha (beginning of any self, autobiography) is not an absolute but originates, as it were, *in medias res.* The first line is interesting in its ambiguity: it names the temporal process of natural growth and suggests the web of causality; yet taken with "Beware of be" it seems a command, a piece of advice. In the third line she rejects the traditional Platonic view, according to which the realm of Being—as distinguished from that of temporal existence—is ideal in its transcendence of all possible realization, and not only ideal ("what no one can be") but invisible and ineffable. "Anybody can say be" is merely a whimsical emphasis of the idea that Being is not ineffable; while "Be is for biography" hints that the Aristotelians are right, as against the Platonists, in affirming that Being (in the sense of ideas and universals, and also in the sense of fullness or depth of reality)

---

3. This whole passage is a good example of Gertrude Stein's deceptive simplicity and nonchalance of style, which often condenses a remarkable complexity of thought.

can be found only in concrete, historical existences and especially in *life*.

But the last three lines, with their careful qualification
with respect to autobiography, bring us to the heart of her
own position. They suggest that to be a *self* is in both senses
a final achievement—"be comes after"—and an achievement
that must be sought repeatedly. In an act that is an act of
freedom because it renounces the obvious impingement of
existence, man must again and again ("once more") discipline himself. He must renounce both "because" (the web of
causal relations to which he normally feels subjected) and
"become" (the realm of time and organic process). We
should note the skillful ambiguity of the final "become." It
may be read as a noun, correlative with "because" (thus
referring to natural becoming), or as an infinitive, correlative with "renounce" (in which case it refers to self-realization). In the light of Gertrude Stein's work as a whole, I
suggest that this act is an act of detachment and genuine
recollection—or what Gabriel Marcel has called "ingatheredness." [4]

This passage is notable for its grasp of a very difficult
problem, and for the candor with which it presents the paradox. For it is a paradox that if, as the traditional Aristotelian
position maintains, being is indissolubly linked with becoming (existence and causality), nevertheless man can reach
self-realization and fullness of being only by forgetting this
linkage. Or does he not only forget but really overcome it?
It is evident that Gertrude Stein wavered on this point. She
habitually rejected all notions of transcendence and eternal

4. *The Mystery of Being*, 2 vols. (Chicago: Henry Regnery Company,
1950), I, 126.

reconciliation; yet she acknowledged in the act of authentic creation, at least, a real disconnection between being and existence, and the emergence from this disconnection of a new depth in reality, a re-collection.

In fact she seems to have thought that this highest activity of the human mind—the act of creative insight—is an interesting special case within the more general order of cosmic creation. She never talks, to be sure, about "being" and "existing" as absolutely discontinuous conditions in reality. But by insisting that there is no relation between the human mind and human nature, she implies that, for man, there is always the possibility of realizing some disconnection between being and existence. How this disconnection occurs is a mystery: it is mysterious because "To know what the human mind is there is no knowing what the human mind is because as it is it is; . . . nobody sees the human mind while it is being existing" (GHA, 104, 146). An analogous mystery is apparent in the advent of newness in the world of species or events—a mystery that modern thinkers cover up too easily with the blanket word "emergence."

Mysterious though it is, the experience of disconnection is not strange to anyone who has ever forgotten himself, lost all self-consciousness in the presence of a great work of art —or in a moment of absorbed intellectual activity. There is a transient integration of the whole of one's being in such a recollected state; and in retrospect, at least, another self seems to have momentarily emerged, as a result of one's detachment from the net of ordinary care, worry, or self-interest. During such moments of focus, time, place, memory, and identity sink into nothingness. It was because time ceases to flow, while one is lost to himself in this way, that Gertrude Stein wrote,

> You need not expect time to be solid.
> You might but you do not have to.
> And as you do not have to you do not. (GHA, 172)

Gertrude Stein denied that time and space are "inside" the human mind; she regarded them as empirical phenomena, just as she regarded memory and identity as dependent upon the empirical self. She maintained that memory (with its freight of the past) interferes with creation. For her, "identity" never means self-realization, which is an achievement of the human mind and belongs to the order of "being." Her "identity," on the contrary, refers to the ground tone of human nature: its tendency toward subjectivity and egotism. Human nature is a part of cosmic existence and the temporal order. Identity is inevitably conferred upon the individual by his external relations (his function in society) and depends upon an audience. Thus she found it amusing to say, "I am I because my little dog knows me," adding, "That does not prove anything about you it only proves something about the dog" (GHA, 75). It is interesting to note that for her, as for Eastern thinkers, identity is a source of distortion and illusion: thus she says again and again that identity, like time, has nothing to do with the human mind.

Nobody knew better than Gertrude Stein did that time is real and can pass. We live, she said, in time and identity but, as we are, we do not know time and identity. In the perspective of existence there is only relative permanence, for change and chance are inexorable. Yet human nature manifests an invincible tendency to repeat itself in relation to a stable environment, so that the determinations of the past predominate: "any day is nevertheless more yesterday than today." The business of living is the realm of relation and necessity; in the activities of daily life, chance is circumstance, and becoming is physical growth and decay. And though common experience is full of chance and contingency, still, insofar as habit and law prevail, ideas are immersed in spatio-temporal orders and assume an almost unbreakable rigidity of pattern.

Regarded in the perspective of being, on the other hand, life is the uncaused self-realization of essences and, instead of habit and law, chance manifests itself as a *fundamental* category. And "chance" seems to mean here, as for Peirce and James, that mysterious indeterminacy in reality which permits real possibility (in the sense of genuine alternatives) and real emergent novelty. But the determinate elements in becoming, in physical growth and decay, have nothing to do directly with real possibility.[5] Time as organic process is solid (a continuum), and it is only when an ideal order supervenes upon experience in a discrete "moment" of the ongoing present that the disconnection between being and existence occurs. Such a moment, created by subjective interest, is a present state. In the present, and the present alone, ideas are disengaged from the matter that fills them and the matter itself is open to new forms. Because the real present

5. See, for example, *What Are Masterpieces,* p. 90. Here Gertrude Stein says: "the boy and the man have nothing to do with each other, except in respect to memory and identity." Thus if the man continues to be (as a personality) what he was as a child, there is no development of real possibility, though he has grown physically.

constitutes a gap, where past and future, idea and actuality, form and matter, are momentarily unhooked, so to speak, and separated, novelty is possible.

Even in the unconscious processes of nature, the present moment wavers; and although there is an overwhelming probability that its contents will assume once more the habit-determined configuration of the past, there is always the possibility of significant change. In human experience, similarly, the real possibility of the "human mind" is latent in each moment. Like the flame on the candle, or the incandescence in electric wires, the human mind—in the special sense of spirit, or inspired perception, which Stein gave this term— is the realized possibility of human existence. It is the manifestation of being, which cannot transcend *all* time but which unites the generations of mankind in the supersensual experience of values. Gertrude Stein believed that the "being existing" of the human mind is intermittent, because human nature is so preoccupying that "entity" (being "with a thing in itself and not in relation") seldom occurs. And though the human mind is always "one," she denied that there could be "a time when all the time the human mind was within which time" (GHA, 149). But "every time there is a human mind it is or it is not all the universe which is or is not (GHA, 124).

The dualistic theory of reality just sketched obviously derives from Gertrude Stein's reflection upon her own experience of the creative act. As Whitehead so frequently pointed out, however, the metaphysician is required not only to look for his broadest general principles within one favored area of experience, but also to test the applicability of these principles to other areas. In her own informal way Gertrude Stein met this requirement with a general theory of cosmology, which it is my purpose now to discuss. The salient point here is her attempt to reconcile an affirmation of possibility and creative purpose (with respect to the human mind) with a thoroughly naturalistic and temporalistic conception of "eternity." The argument turns upon the notions of chance and the infinite past (and future) duration of the cosmos.

We know that, in time, determinate things disappear or are transformed into something else, that there is a real discontinuity between being and existing, for individuals die but the world goes on. There are naturally some things that go on all the time, and some things that go on only from time to time. The things that go on all the time make the universe, where as the things that go on from time to time make history and biography. The things that go on all the time, like birth and death, the cycle of the seasons, the rising and setting of the sun, are natural events which by their regularity preserve an ordered and dynamic universe. But there are also things that appear only once and do not "continue": they "come to stay." They become free from time, though they appear in time and endure through time.

Such are the masterpieces of art, Gertrude Stein said; and she might have added, as she does by implication, such are the lives of saints, which are really masterpieces of experience. Both are works of what Gabriel Marcel calls "creative fidelity." Marcel defines faithfulness as

the active recognition of something permanent, not formally, after the manner of a law, but ontologically; in this sense, it refers invariably to a presence, or to something which can be maintained within us and before us as a presence, but which, *ipso facto,* can be just as well ignored, forgotten, and obliterated; and this reminds us of the menace of betrayal which, to my mind, overshadows the whole world.[6]

Like the saint, who by the practice of the presence of God is faithful to *presence* more than to anything else, masterpieces are acts of creative fidelity which affirm life in the face of the knowledge of death. They enter into the existential universe and are subject to the vicissitudes of time in that they can be destroyed or lost. (In this connection, however, we must remember how lasting are the products of human culture and how their meaning endures: the oldest human writing has been deciphered.) Yet in one sense—a very special sense and, in spite of Gertrude Stein's incomplete Platonism, a very Platonic sense—masterpieces become part of the things that "go on." They persist; but not as do the broad recurrences and regularities of the existential world. In a masterpiece, being and existence are no longer capable of disconnection: the work is an end in itself and (so long as it exists at all) it always exists in the same form and with the same content, although we may change in our feelings toward it.

In her theory of masterpieces Gertrude Stein thus makes a significant concession to the concept of the eternal; and in acknowledging that great art is an end in itself, she seems to represent timeless perfection as the goal of time. It would be a mistake to suppose, however, that she conceived of the existential universe as in any way guided by creative purpose. In the temporal process, the motions of things that "go on all the time" are incapable, in their slowly changing regu-

6. "On the Ontological Mystery," *The Philosophy of Existence* (New York: Philosophical Library, 1949), p. 21.

larities, of the free perfection of individual acts. For her, there is a constant movement in time, but there is no progressing—if, that is, progress implies destiny, for there is no goal to which change draws nearer, beyond the movement itself. There can be no teleology in the time processes because—since time is infinite—there is no final *point d'appui*. There can only be endless restlessness and becoming: the fundamental maxim is merely that you cannot step twice into the same river.

If time is infinite, eternity has, for the cosmos as a whole, no other meaning than everlastingness, and the universe looks neither forward nor backward nor "elsewhere" for perfection. Passage and action realize space, which is without boundaries, so far as we know; it has no center and no periphery. And yet a finite universe exists in the spatio-temporal continuum, dynamically sustained in equilibrium throughout the whole at every moment of time. But Gertrude Stein says that "the things that move do not make the universe," but that the universe and the human mind "fly around" and that "If anything flies around there is no ending and no begun" (GHA, 139, 141). Here, I believe, is another statement of the paradox involved in the pairing of being and existence which cosmogony and teleology seek to explain.

This finite universe, whose limits we do not know, exists and has its being in the spatio-temporal continuum. The possible universes that might have been are no longer possible, for this is the one that actually is. If time is open at both ends, and if the universe is always determinate in some way in space, then the universe has always existed as some kind of ordered whole. Thus, regarding infinite possibility, the universe is limited by what it contains. Insofar as it endures in infinite time, it can be said to contain infinite possibilities —but these are drastically limited at any actual time. Although the universe changes, therefore, it can never change to another universe. There is no need for either a cosmogony or a teleology.

Since Gertrude Stein believed that in this universe being and existence are not *necessarily* related (the present moment providing the possibility of their disconnection and of new forms), she quite logically believed that chance is the fundamental category of existence. In fact she was fond of saying that nothing is known of the word "necessary." She points out, for example, that there is no law requiring one to be born, and no law governing the habits of the various species of creatures that dwell upon this planet. But, though the content of experience differs at every moment, there are regularities and broad recurrences of patterns. To be born is to be second to our parents; since life does go on, something does follow something else in the continuity of the whole, but without necessity in terms of any individual existence. Contingency, therefore, inheres in the structure of the universe, and chance is an element entering into every regularity and recurrence as its ground. Thus experience is full of surprises because anything that can happen may or may not happen. But something must always happen.[7] This prin-

7. The student of contemporary philosophy will perceive that this view that nothing in particular is necessitated, but that something must always happen, is very close to the position of Alfred North Whitehead. The question of influence is not very interesting, although Whitehead and Gertrude Stein were good friends. But if the great philosopher's cosmology influenced Gertrude Stein's world view, it is equally possible that her own enthusiasm for emergent novelty and creativeness (especially in the arts) helped Whitehead to shape his own aesthetic views, as well as his vision of creativity and its "creative advance."

ciple that "something must always happen" is directly related to the assumption that the past and future of the
cosmos are infinite. Both ideas derive inescapably from the
fundamental Aristotelian assumption that possibility and
being are linked to and dependent on existence.

Thus Gertrude Stein can say that "any little thing is how
it was begun" and that "something always takes a long time"
(GHA, 191, 63) without implying any necessity for existence and without contradicting the idea that the spatio-
temporal continuum neither begins nor ends. In other words,
she does not say that anything can come from nothing. As a
time concept, negation means simply that something that
might or might not exist does not exist at a given time and
place. As a space concept, negation means that something
that might or might not exist does not in fact exist anywhere
now—a kind of negation, of course, that cannot be proved.
Regarding existence, a man can only affirm what is; he cannot really deny what is not, except in relation to time and
place. "Nothing," in short, cannot be opposed either to "being" or to the existential order.

For Gertrude Stein, then, the universe drifts continually
into different chance configurations which exclude and dictate certain possibilities for its configurations of the future.
Some of these configurations may be really "new," and some
may be accidental repetitions: in neither case are they a
manifestation of cosmic purpose. When they occur, however,
they take their place in the existential order; since they have
proved to be possible, their place is guaranteed by the continuity of the whole. Whatever appears new to us, in any
case, appears so only because it contradicts some familiar
and established pattern. In the recurrence of the old and the

occurrence of the new, chance plays an equally important role; but we do not notice it except when we confront the unexpected, which may in fact be new or old. Chance is possible because being is not related necessarily in any one way to becoming. But chance does not sever all connection between being and existing; it merely refers to the possible discontinuities between them.

Although Gertrude Stein always welcomes the advent of novelty and the challenge of the unexpected, her deepest emphasis is actually on possibility and on creativeness. In her life, moreover, she conveyed her vision in a way which seems to have liberated people, making them feel that the "new" was able to come to birth in them, and through them. (No doubt few people ever worked out the subtlety of her thought on this subject. It was probably communicated by the direct impact of her personality and her witty conversation.)

But what did this idea of "creation," or "creativeness," mean to Gertrude Stein? It is clear that, whatever else "creation" means in her philosophical vocabulary, it does not imply a cosmogony; it does not refer to the creation of the universe *ex nihilo*. She does not posit a primal chaos without any kind of regularity, and no original nullity in the sense of absolute zero. She talks a great deal about "nothing." But this nothing of which she speaks is equal to everything and anything—the totality of what is and what can be. "Nothing" is not a something that antedates time and space; it is the germinal possibility within things that exist in time and space. Nothing is really everything, and whether it becomes *anything* (that is, a concrete emergent novelty) depends upon realization. As the widest generality, however, "Nothing can grow" (GHA, 118): something new can appear (although it need not) that is second to nothing in the causal chain.

"In the beginning," therefore, is an existential concept and always concerns individuals. To begin *in time* can refer only to particular existents, and every existent is second to something else in the causal sequence. In the order of existence, everyone puts in an appearance for the first time and enters into time processes: "Nothing should follow something because in this way there will come to be a middle and a beginning and an end and of course that does make identity but not the human mind or not the human mind" (GHA, 117). In the order of being, on the contrary, there is no such necessary sequence and no beginning, for the human mind is the "whole" of all possible knowledge, just as the universe is the whole of all possible existents, and neither is ever fully realized at any one time.

Gertrude Stein believed that our ideas are grounded in an objective, existential world, but that they have their being in the realm of possibility. She implies that if there were no geography, no geographical history, there would be no human mind (GHA, 31-32). But she insists that "geography does not look like it does in relation to the human mind" (GHA, 26)—that the ideal orders which constitute the unity of the human mind are timeless possibilities in human experience and have their being independent of any one. The universal, therefore, has nothing to do with a universe. As James said, "the mere existence of things to be known is even now not, as a rule, sufficient to bring about a knowledge of them. Our abstract and general discoveries usually come to us as lucky fancies; and it is only *après coup* that we find that they correspond to some reality." [8]

With respect to any individual, the "nothing" that follows something (his particular existence) need realize no idea that others have not already realized before him: he may never differentiate himself from others of his kind in the ways he responds to experience, although his experience is his own and his responses are his own. In such a one, "being" and "existing" are disconnected only at birth and death; his life is lived in time and identity. Original creation, on the other hand, is never a becoming. In the cosmos generally, original creation may manifest itself, for example, in the advent of a new form or species; and insofar as it is an event of *origination* it owes its unique character to the momentary unhooking of being and existence—followed by the unforeseen realization of a new possibility. In human experience, too, original creation is the result of realization, or decision, after a moment of discontinuity during which some old connection between ideas is ruptured and a new relation spontaneously generated. Such decisions are made, in utter independence of the causal chain, by the "human mind." They are manifestations of the primary function of the human mind and are connected with time processes—although not caused by them—because from time to time the human mind can decide what anything is:

Every once in so often is every once in so often and anybody can decide what nothing is.

8. *The Principles of Psychology*, 2 vols. (New York: Henry Holt and Company, 1910), II, 630-631.

Please excuse me.

If nothing is anything any one every once in so often can decide what anything is.

That is the way it is. (GHA, 123-124)

These decisions are the only real "beginnings." They are made in the real present—the Now of detachment from personal identity and time processes per se. They have to do with what is, what goes on, and they are determined by nothing beyond themselves. They can be connected with anything, however, for they regard the whole universe. The universe is thus a hieroglyph which man deciphers in two ways: by living his life in it and by knowing it. And knowing it means experiencing it, not as a process in time, but as a manifold of actualities and possibilities. Realization requires space and time in nature; but creative realization, in the human mind, requires only "presence," in which being rises superior to existence. For "presence," particular times and places are only accidentally involved in the spontaneous mental act of vision. One either begins or begins again, in his effort to be faithful to the "being existing" that is latent within him.

Gertrude Stein's recurrent meditations on the creative realizations or decisions of the human mind are not far from Jacques Maritain's conception of creative intuition. Like Maritain, she was opposed to surrealism's irrational surrender to the unconscious; like him (although her own work was sometimes branded, erroneously, as automatic writing), she realized that

automatism "unbinds that which had been brought to the unity of life by concentration," and by that brooding repose of the soul which we call in French *recueillement*. Automatism does not produce freedom, but only dispersion. Separated from intellectual light, the automatic life of the unconscious is fundamentally unable to reveal anything really *new*.[9]

It was for some such reason as this that she told Kate Buss there was no real barrier between her thinking and unthinking mind—a claim which (though doubtless exaggerated) certainly makes clear her conception of what is ideally desirable in the creative process. Therefore we also find in all her discussions of the creative act an emphasis on the clear light of intelligence: the act is a decision, an interpretation, a realization, of the human *mind*.

Yet Stein always insists with equal emphasis on faithfulness to one's own latent "being existing," and here I think she is very close to existentialism's concept of the *authentic*. For her, as for the existentialist, the creative act is never an act of the detached rational intelligence: the inner depths of the creator are involved. Although she was hostile to the Freudian attempt to explain, or explain away, the creative impulse in terms of the (Freudian) unconscious, she would no doubt have agreed with Maritain in his belief that genuine creation is largely the product of a "spiritual unconscious or preconscious," which is the matrix where our deepest decisions and commitments of will are prepared and whence emerge our most fertile ideas, our most significant perceptions, our most beautiful intellectual solutions.[10] In any case, she claimed to have dispensed with ordinary memory and discursive reasoning in much of her own work, apparently relying on a highly disciplined power of immediate, intuitive perception. And it is out of such perception,

9. Jacques Maritain, *Creative Intuition in Art and Poetry* (New York: Pantheon Press, 1953), p. 81.
10. Maritain, pp. 91-94.

she believed, that the masterpiece is conceived and formed.

But when the mind has the vitality to sustain such deep perceptions persistently, and the energy then to create enduring and significant forms, one must speak of "genius." Gertrude Stein did speak of "genius," repeatedly. In fact she often gives the impression that—like Proust and Joyce—she exalted genius and its works a little too highly: "the rest," she once observed, "is just there anyway" (EA, 118). In her theory of genius, moreover, in spite of her hostility to the concept of the unconscious, she seems not unlike Poincaré, who speaks of "unconscious work," or F. W. H. Myers, who thought it was the habitual yet unexpected incursion of a "subliminal Self." Her own expression is the "flash of lightning" (EA, 120); and in one passage she exclaims, "I wish I knew how I did it" (HTW, 108). Thus like every theory of inspiration that comes from authentic experience, her own bears witness to the unexpected advent—the surprise.

There is apparently a contradiction between Gertrude Stein's view of genius and her belief that "being existing," or the human mind, is the latent possibility of human existence generally. (The very fact that she calls it the *human* mind implies this kind of universality.) But this contradiction is as old as humanity itself. Even Christianity, with its doctrines of grace and the spirit that "bloweth where it listeth," seems to express a similar insight—with respect to sanctity, of course, rather than secular creativeness. Certainly Gertrude Stein was grimly, though compassionately, aware of the appalling rarity of that fortunate combination of circumstance and vital endowment which makes genius possible. Concerning the vast majority of human beings, she said that the struggle for existence leaves them so little surplus energy that only rarely are they capable of living in the human mind.

In spite of this pessimism (well justified in the light of actual experience), she does have a word of practical wisdom to offer us. True, she expects only talented and fortunate young people to be able to profit by it. She often observed that it was useless to expect anything much of people over thirty. But this final advice of hers is traditional in its depth. The creative beginning, she tells us—the beginning in which "Nothing can grow"—is always an act of inwardness. And judging from her comments, one feels that it is an act which, though inaccessible to the majority because of limited endowment and circumstance, is nonetheless in some sense natural to man. Here, I think, the very sturdiness of her empiricism forces her into a view that is more Platonic than was her intention:

Just begin with within that is do not begin, no do not begin, how can anyone begin when within is not cannot be begun. Just be reasonable about this, please do. (GHA, 157)

This passage has a Platonic (or Vedantic?) ring because the intuition that "within is not cannot be begun" implies an eternal depth, an eternal dimension, in man. Moreover, it is an intuition that seems to come inevitably to people who are profound in their experience of recollection. According to Gabriel Marcel, who has given this experience so much thought, recollection is hard to define because

it transcends the dualism of being and action, or, more correctly, because it reconciles in itself these two aspects of the antinomy. The word means what it says—the act whereby I re-collect myself as a unity; but this hold, this grasp upon myself, is also relaxation

and abandon. *Abandon to . . . relaxation in the presence of . . .*
—yet there is no noun for these prepositions to govern. The way
stops at the threshold . . . It is within recollection that I take my
position . . . in regard to my life . . . *In this withdrawal I carry
with me that which I am and which perhaps my life is not.* This
brings out the gap between my being and my life. I am not my
life.[11]

Marcel is groping here, with his usual sensitivity, to express certain nuances of this deep experience, which has
given rise to many different religious and metaphysical attitudes. His conclusions are not those of Gertrude Stein, but
one is almost forced to suppose that she had touched, again
and again, this "gap" of which he speaks—the gap between
being and life, between the human mind and human nature,
between something eternal and something time-bound. In
the following passage she is defining this very gap, but with
her customary distrust of transcendence and reconciliation
she makes of it an even sharper problem:

Not solve it but be in it, that is what one can say of the problem
of the relation of human nature to the human mind, which does
not exist because there is none there is no relation, because when
you are in the human mind you are in it, and when you are in
human nature you are of it. (GHA, 155-156)

It seems to me that there are at least three significant links
between Gertrude Stein's philosophy and her actual achievement as a writer. To begin with, the split she insisted on between human nature and the human mind led her away from
conventional fiction (whose material is largely human nature

11. *Philosophy of Existence*, pp. 12-13. The first two series of dots in the
quotation are in the original; the others are my ellipses.

and its life history)—away from events and the natural spatio-temporal sequences of ordinary experience—into verbalized "illustrations" of the interior life of mind, which ultimately culminated in something more properly called *meditations*. Second, her ontological reflections are paralleled, in a precise and interesting way, by her reflections upon the nature of language itself. Finally, I wish to suggest that her conception of "being existing," and her theory that novelty and creative vision are a consequence of the moment of discontinuity between being and existence, stem from the root experience which produced her most curiously vital and yet often unintelligible writing. If I am correct, this root experience was the serious practice of meditation—and not merely meditation but, at times, genuine *recollection*. These points need further development.

Gertrude Stein tells us that there was a time when she was concerned only with temporal beginnings and continuities—that is, with life (its growth and decay) and with human nature and psychology. She ultimately left this preoccupation, however, in quest of a "reality that has nothing to do with the passage of time" and could say, "Now I am writing about what is which is being existing" (EA, 154, 251). A brief glance at the chronology of her work bears out this statement.

Scientific completeness combines with psychological insight and rare sensitivity of observation in the stories of *Three Lives* (written in 1904-1905). The same qualities are developed in her monumental novel, or "history of a family's progress," *The Making of Americans* (written in 1906-1908). Composed in a kind of basic English and revealing an ear for speech rhythms as keen as Mark Twain's, these works are merely an extension of ordinary naturalistic fiction—dealing primarily with the flow of time and its erosions (although one could say much more than this) and with time's deposits, in the human psyche, of habit and bondage. Their intention is thoroughly scientific, to classify and differentiate psychological types: "I was sure that in a kind of a way the enigma of the universe could in this way be solved. That after all description is explanation, and if I went on and on enough I could describe every individual human being that could possibly exist. I did proceed to do as much as I could" (LIA, 142).

Except for a certain dullness, coming from a repetitious style and a lack of plot, neither *Three Lives* nor *The Making of Americans* presents any real difficulty to the reader. But while completing *The Making of Americans* and in the midst of yet another work of this kind, *A Long Gay Book* (1909), she began to lose faith in science and to experiment with a very different and less intelligible kind of writing—the composition of what she called "portraits." It was in 1909 that she wrote "Ada," the first of her separate portraits and a definite break with the earlier fiction. In the next few years she was to complete *Tender Buttons*, a curious set of apparently unintelligible yet sometimes strangely beautiful poems. Meanwhile, and later, she was writing more portraits, the purpose of each being to express the "bottom nature" of an individual without recourse to either narrative or description. She would silently put a question to the person—such as "How do you like what you have?"—and then try to put into words the quality of the life force she sensed in him: "I must find out what is moving inside them that makes them them, and I must find out how I by the thing moving excitedly in me can make a portrait of them" (LIA, 183).

Later, along with the portraits, she composed a number of plays—perhaps the most fertile year with respect to variety being 1927, in which not only *Four Saints in Three Acts* appeared but also *Lucy Church Amiably,* which she called a "novel of romantic beauty." The 1930s brought her a wider public, with the appearance of the two autobiographies and her lectures and essays, all of which are easy enough to read and often delightfully funny. But this final period is really dominated by *The Geographical History of America,* which Thornton Wilder has characterized in his introduction as "a book that says what it knows; a work of philosophy, a work of art, and a work of gaiety."

In spite of the enigmatic quality of much of this later writing, it is alive with suggestion, occasional drollery, and freshness of feeling and perception. But though some of it purports to be fiction or drama, there is an important sense in which all of it is pure meditation: that is, it is devoted to the human mind and its responses and realizations—and to a vision of the world in "being existing." For instance, *Four Saints* is a charming opera, but concerning it she wrote, "I wanted the sentiment of doing nothing invented by myself" (EA, 283)—and the sentiment of doing nothing is hardly material for a conventional plot. This meditative quality persists in her subsequent work in which there is again at least a minimum of recognizable action: *Ida,* for example, and *Mrs. Reynolds* (in which Stein said there was nothing historical "except the state of mind"), as well as *Doctor Faustus Lights the Lights* and *The Mother of Us All.*

The development of the meditative element in Gertrude Stein's work was associated from the very beginning, 1909 or 1910, with her search for creative language. In her career, indeed, we find a deepening preoccupation with "what is" (with "being existing" and the revelations of the human mind) paralleled by an increasing absorption in linguistic experiments—one might almost call it an obsession with language in and for itself, with the need for restoring to exhausted words and phrases their original freshness and wonder. In fact, twenty-five years of this kind of working and playing with language preceded the publication of *The Geographical History of America,* the mature summary of her reflections upon "what is" and what "can be." Thus in a way her convictions about the nature of "being existing" seem to have grown out of her linguistic work. At least, to the close student of her later writing, it is clear that she had perceived that deep linkage between language and being which emerges for anyone who ponders very long upon language.[12]

Heidegger, for example, tells us that language is the very "dwelling place of being." In her own way Gertrude Stein (though she believed that ideas and words are not the same thing) would have agreed with this: throughout her work, after the publication of *Tender Buttons* in 1914, there runs a persistent concern with language, the writer's medium,

12. Gertrude Stein apparently composed a number of pieces in an effort to determine whether or not one can write words in such a fashion that meaning is absolutely absent. She concluded (although many of her readers will disagree with her) that this cannot be done. Carl Van Vechten, in his introduction to *Selected Writings of Gertrude Stein* (New York: Random House, 1946), has expressed the belief that "someone completely familiar with the routine, and roundabout, way of Miss Stein's daily life would be able to explain every line of her prose" (p. xiv). In the preface to *Bee Time Vine,* Virgil Thomson classifies the poems in the collection in three groups: those which are "clear as Kipling"; those which, like "Lifting Belly," depend upon an acquaintance with Stein's daily life; and those which are abstract compositions, or "genuinely hermetic," in which no discernible parallel to common sense can be found in the meaning of the words.

which she came to regard as the greatest of all mediums because it alone embodies, and fosters, the human mind's perceptions of immaterial values. And as late as 1931 she was writing: "There are two things a dictionary and a country" (HTW, 19).

In context this remark is only another variation on her great theme of the dichotomy between human nature and the human mind. For while human nature is the manifestation of causality and becoming in the individual, the country is the fundamental objective source of possibility in social and historical existence—the primary condition which affects human nature or upon which human nature operates. Thus her complete analogy may be translated as follows: as the country stands in relation to human nature (temporal existence), so stands language in relation to the human mind ("being existing"). The word is an inexhaustible symbol, a reservoir of possible extensions of meaning in experience. It is by profound attention to words in old and significant contexts—the thought and literature of the past—that the human mind feeds and strengthens itself. And old words in new contexts are capable of expressing the really new experience, or the new perception of value.

It is significant, however, that Gertrude Stein speaks here not of language as it is written or spoken, but of the *dictionary*. In speech and writing alike, the context delimits the meaning of the words and determines it, there, once and for all. She saw clearly that the incessant practical use—in the service of greedy human nature—has exhausted the spoken word and its printed substitutes, especially in our time; although the sources of language may be lost in depth and miracle, its useful adaptations have always tended to reduce it to either empty chatter or mere signaling. But as words stand in the dictionary, dissociated from every context, they exhibit to the imaginative mind the full spectrum of their powers and possibilities.

Gertrude Stein wrote many essays on language, at times undervaluing words in behalf of her effort to distinguish between name and nature and in order to "see" things rather than words, but she never developed explicitly the implications of this dimension of the possibility in words. Much of her linguistic commentary deals with grammar, showing that the grammatical structure of language has been developed largely in the service of human nature's needs and desires. This is a logical conclusion for a naturalist to arrive at; it is also probably very true, as far as it goes. For as Philip Wegener recognized more than fifty years ago, language as a structure must have grown up by emendation—that is, by *pointing* (verbal or otherwise) and making the context clear. The intellectual structure of grammar and its severe logical power, then, are the outgrowth of a very practical (though probably unconscious) process. But if we disregard grammatical structure and consider words as such, we see that words can "vibrate"; that they sometimes exhibit overtones and levels of meaning; and that in the perception of such levels and vibrations the human mind itself is manifested. Gertrude Stein paid little attention, in her theoretical discussions, to this aspect of language, perhaps because it seemed to her merely another result of discontinuity—a result as inexplicable as the emergence of "being existing" in the midst of temporal becoming.

In her literary practice, however, Stein came to pay a great deal of attention to this. If we study her work carefully we can see that from 1910 on, at least, it was her purpose to exhibit words afresh: to dissociate them from conventional context and stale association, and thus to display them with more of their power and capacity for vibration—more, in short, of their *being*. Now vibration occurs when a word conveys simultaneously two or more of its possible meanings, each of which is relevant to the context—a control of meaning that is, of course, strictly dependent on the context itself. Like the creation of metaphor,[13] the ability to make words vibrate is one of the great poetic gifts. (We are much indebted to William Empson for making us aware of this resonance in English poetry.) And the poet's work not only conserves and restores language, but startles the receptive reader into a fresh awareness of his own mind. If the dictionary, then, serves as a dwelling place of possibility, it is creative writing that is the real dwelling place of being (or, for Gertrude Stein, of "being existing").

Her purpose was to wrench the word from its groove in custom and habit. I think she also meant to place it (by setting it so strangely in a strange context) under a kind of magnifying glass—perhaps even a burning glass that would kindle it anew. In *The Geographical History* she has the following illuminating passage:

I found that any kind of a book if you read with glasses and somebody is cutting your hair and so you cannot keep the glasses on and you use your glasses as a magnifying glass and so read

13. It is irrelevant to discuss metaphor here, since Gertrude Stein was singularly indifferent to it. Though naturally her work contains a good deal of metaphorical extension, she was more concerned with the concrete, literal meaning of words—and far more concerned with the revival of a word's full meaning. Her finest metaphors are actually a revival of the latent metaphor (inherent but often forgotten) in the ordinary word. She does not try to create "figures of speech."

word by word reading word by word makes the writing that is not anything be something. (GHA, 115)

The image conveys aptly that sense of a word's import (and real "being") which emerges when one magnifies it by pausing to look with deep attentiveness at the word itself, and not at its limited meaning in a limited context.

It is in flashes like this magnifying-glass passage, not in elaborated essays, that Gertrude Stein rounds out for us her theory of language. The same passage, however, is also an apt image for her general ontological theory. The visual "break" on the page made by the magnifying glass suggests vividly the moment of discontinuity between being and existence; the sudden enlargement suggests that emergence of novelty or inspired perception, which discontinuity permits throughout reality as a whole. The implicit analogy, therefore, runs like this: as the enhanced power of the word stands to the grammatical structure and stale associations from which the word is now dissociated, so stands the moment of discontinuity in "being existing" to those conditions of existence to which it rises superior.

This subtle combination of apparently disparate ideas suggests long and fruitful meditation, but it also suggests a significant root experience as the origin or center of Gertrude Stein's insights. To be sure, it seems clear that for many years she engaged in the serious practice of meditation, and in a sense not far from that in which "meditation" has been traditionally understood. But meditation as such will not explain the significance of discontinuity in Gertrude Stein's view of "being existing"; nor will it illuminate the connection between her ontology and her linguistic theory and purpose. As I have said before, the root experience we are seeking, I believe, was a genuine experience of recollection—what Marcel calls "ingatheredness," or real contemplation.

There is testimony to the fact that she practiced meditation. Thornton Wilder, who knew her well in her later years, tells us in his introduction to *Four in America* that Gertrude Stein had an impressive habit of meditating every day. He makes it clear, however, that he speaks of meditating in the sense of rigorously pursuing a certain train of thought for an hour or two at a time; and he does not tell us whether her meditations ever carried her over the psychic border, so to speak, into what Marcel means by contemplation. But in the same introduction he also says: "It has often seemed to me that Miss Stein was engaged in a series of spiritual exercises whose aim was to eliminate during the hours of writing all those whispers into the ear from the outside and inside world where audience dwells" (xiii). Wilder is not, of course, telling us that Gertrude Stein was a religious mystic, although his words suggest a purgative effort, not unlike that of the mystic or yogin, directed toward creative authenticity. He is speaking, however, of a disciplined technique of *waiting*, which if successful is accompanied by the promptings of "inspiration." Concerning this phenomenon Gertrude Stein said: "One may really indeed say that that is the essence of genius . . . that is being one who is at the same time talking and listening" (LIA, 170). But to reach this point of detachment from an audience (including one's own human nature), one must "renounce because and become"—an act so difficult, and attended with so much sacrifice of the ego, that "the human mind is like not being in danger but being killed" (GHA, 28). This kind of contemplation is no doubt exceedingly rare, especially in our extroverted, mechanized age.

Yet it is as natural to the artist as to the mystic, if he fulfills his vocation. (Marcel makes this marvelously clear when he defines the contemplative act as a "turning inwards of our awareness of the outer world." [14])

Contemplation at any level worth discussing is always accompanied by a moment of *dissociation,* psychologically speaking, or of *alienation.* Such dissociation belongs to a larger group of psychic phenomena, some of which are normal and others pathological. Sleep is a perfectly normal form, frequently accompanied by dreaming. So is a certain drowsy state preceding sleep, often marked by hypnogogic phenomena such as interior voices or vivid visions. Dissociation is pathological, of course, not only in psychosis as such but also in all kinds of mediumistic phenomena, including multiple personality and automatic writing. In these cases, because of some defect in personality structure, reason is unable to dominate and judge those visions, voices, impulses, or ideas which are presented by the dissociated (and unconscious) segment of the psyche.[15] Creative dissociation, or contemplation, must be distinguished from these other forms by the intelligent, disciplined effort that has prepared for it and by the harvest of valid intuitions that the trained and unified unconscious mind presents, as a result, to consciousness.[16]

I believe that Gertrude Stein experienced such creative

14. *Mystery of Being,* I, 126.
15. For an excellent discussion of these forms of alienation, see E. Récéjac, *Essay on the Bases of the Mystic Knowledge* (New York, 1899), pp. 158-163.
16. That the harvest of this kind of attention is inspiration—and surprising insight—has been attested by men of genius in many fields. But people who are by no means "geniuses" sometimes almost accidentally touch the fringes of the experience.

dissociation frequently, to a fairly marked degree, and that she forged her distinctively personal philosophy out of reflection upon it. The chief emphasis of her mature thought, as we have seen, is on the moment of discontinuity throughout reality and on the enhanced "being existing" that then emerges. Thus she persistently links habit and greed with bondage and the noncreative; the moment of detachment, with freedom and creative perception. She might have acquired these insights through reflective reading and her experience of life. But their recurrence everywhere in her work argues an extraordinary preoccupation—as well as firsthand acquaintance with the condition in which "the human mind is being existing." For it is in periods of deep and self-forgetful contemplation that one oftenest encounters not only new constellations of form and meaning in the materials presented to the mind, but also new depths of power and creativeness accessible to oneself.

Similarly, the experience of creative dissociation seems related to Stein's attempt to dissociate words from their trite or formal contexts. Very likely she first discovered the connection between levels of mental detachment and levels of verbal spontaneity and "being" in the course of her earliest attempts at a new kind of writing. It was during the period of the never-completed *Long Gay Book,* and before she began *Tender Buttons,* that she first tried to look again at commonplace objects, scenes, and people—in the effort to register the precise nuances of perception and name them with a unique word or phrase. Such an effort inevitably involves holding the mind very still, in rejection of (or inattention to) every solicitation of the commonplace and every prompting from human nature in its desire to impress an "audience." It was probably here, in an unusually rigorous search for the unique quality and the exact word to name it, that she first stumbled onto a very old spiritual discipline: that introverted waiting which, in Marcel's words, is both a "turning inwards of our awareness of the outer world" and a "kind of inward regrouping of one's resources."

If recollection is the buried link between poetry and thought, for Gertrude Stein, this fact ought to shed some light on the nature and value of her achievement in both fields. It would be easy, I suppose, to criticize her philosophy for a certain inconsistency or irrationality at its core. Yet it might be very difficult to prove that the real universe is any more rational or consistent than the picture one gets from studying *The Geographical History of America*. Although the purposeless, chance-directed cosmos Gertrude Stein assumes seems incapable of accounting for the miracle of "being existing" and the "human mind," still it does provide holes, so to speak, through which an unexplained creative purpose can manifest itself. And this is thoroughly consonant with our experience.

Gertrude Stein's real concern, however, is not to explain the world, but to describe or inspire the *act of presence* by means of which the human mind and cosmic beauty are simultaneously realized. Perhaps, then, her emphasis on a seemingly groundless act is the right emphasis after all: the significant point is that even in her philosophic writing she does demand and evoke from her readers an active creative effort. Thus her deepest ideas are merely suggested—condensed in gnomic phrases or flashed out in a pregnant juxtaposition of ideas—but never rigorously elaborated with any view to helping the reader. In all this she seems oddly akin to those Eastern sages who refuse to explain the disaster of existence and yet make the severest demands on those disciples who would obtain salvation.

It would seem reasonable to assume that her poetic "meditations" make the same aloof demand; that they will reward the reader's effort with the same veiled yet ultimately satisfying coherence. The fact is that this has not been the assumption of either her hostile critics or her most fervent admirers. These groups have disagreed sharply over the value of such writing as *Tender Buttons*, which is an early example, and a crucial one, of her poetic rather than philosophic meditations. But they have all agreed with surprising unanimity on the fundamental unintelligibility of this kind of writing. Thus critics who dislike her work charge that it is either automatic writing[17] or at best a purely subjective outpouring, which has no literary value because it is emptied of communicable meaning. On the other hand, Donald Sutherland, who certainly admires her work, says that *Tender Buttons* does not "mean" anything in the ordinary sense of that word and goes on to make a virtue of this limitation. The book is, he suggests, a deliberately constructed verbal parallel to cubist painting—that is, although the writing stems from real observations or experience, all realistic denotation has been suppressed or dislocated so that

17. This was the view of B. F. Skinner in "Has Gertrude Stein a Secret?" *Atlantic Monthly* (January 1934), pp. 50-57, and it has cropped up frequently in facetious newspaper reviews. No serious critic has entertained it, however, and Gertrude Stein of course denied it (see EA, 267). If her denial is not wholly unequivocal, the reason probably is that the subtle yet crucial distinction between automatic and creative activities of the unconscious mind must have seemed to her to be too factual a point to make in any apologia of her work. The difference should be clear to any sensitive reader: if it is not, the scientific point is wasted.

what remains is an aesthetic surface of pure (and untranslatable) verbal intensity.[18]

If the experience of recollection is the key to Gertrude Stein, however, it is probable that some of her most puzzling and original work drives its fascination from a kind of fusion of intense unconscious activity with a conscious purpose definable in terms not unlike those Sutherland uses. Not only *Tender Buttons* but much of her later work could be described as a conscious attempt to seize the uniqueness of certain fleeting intuitions and, at the same time, to affirm their universality; and when one deals with such a penumbra of quality, there is no fixed vocabulary to use. Her goal in poetry, then, was the "new word." But along with this conscious search we may assume a deeply recollected state. This is not to say, of course, that all of her meditations after *Tender Buttons* were written as a result of recollection. (Some of this work may be contrived—concocted out of erudition, skill, and cleverness—and she delighted in chance associations as well as in dissociations.) I do believe, though, that in *Tender Buttons* Gertrude Stein derived her guiding themes and basic inspiration from moments (however scattered) of profound focus and receptivity. In her later poetry, I think, she sought (and sometimes reached) the same recollectedness, whether her literary goal was always the new word, in this special sense, or not.

The result is an achievement unique in modern writing. No doubt the total volume of Stein's work belongs to the phenomenology of mind rather than to literature: in her effort to grasp and set down her moments of concentrated vision she failed again and again, and she published her failures along with her successes. But her method of discipline

18. *Gertrude Stein,* pp. 71-99, 112-113.

was contemplation—involving creative dissociation; her conscious goal was the new word to express a new and purified perception of common reality. Given these clues, one may expect to find extraordinary riches (both psychological and linguistic) in many hitherto baffling passages. Although creative dissociation does not lead to automatism, nonetheless it does induce an intense activity of the unconscious—if the unconscious has already been "brought to the unity of life," as Maritain puts it, by a state of brooding concentration. It is well known with what incredible flexibility and intricacy of design, under such conditions, the unconscious is able to support and enrich the conscious mind's creative purpose.

Gertrude Stein's conscious purpose was verbal, not mystical in any religious sense. It need not surprise us, therefore, that her unconscious daemon often aided her with all that subtle and witty grasp of linguistic relationships and depth of verbal meaning which is perhaps the prize gift of every man's unconscious mind. The strange vitality with which some of her most interesting passages vibrate, however, seems especially due to the phenomenon of "overdetermination" of meaning—the susceptibility of a given word or phrase to multiple interpretation. This is one of the chief hallmarks of unconscious activity, whether neurotic or creative. And the reader often finds one strange conjunction in particular: a seemingly trivial perception, or a pointed but unimportant flash of wit, linked verbally with a murmured suggestion of ritual, prayer, purgation, and renewal. Is it fanciful to point out that Gertrude Stein was rather more of a genuine sage, if not a frustrated mystic, than she cared to admit? These claims must be examined more closely in the next chapter and substantiated by close analysis of *Tender Buttons*.

Socrates: I should imagine that the name Hermes has to do with speech, and signifies that he is the interpreter (hermēneus), or messenger, or thief, or liar, or bargainer; all that sort of thing has a great deal to do with language. —Plato, Cratylus (408)

South, south which is a wind is not rain, does silence choke speech or does it not.
Lying in a conundrum, lying so makes the springs restless, lying so is a reduction, not lying so is arrangeable.
Releasing the oldest auction that is the pleasing some still renewing.
—Gertrude Stein, Tender Buttons

III. SELFHOOD AND THE WORD:
REFLECTIONS ON *TENDER BUTTONS*

First published in 1914 by the Claire Marie Press, New York, Gertrude Stein's *Tender Buttons* is still regarded (by those who know about it at all) merely as one of the minor curiosities of the poetry renaissance. The book received little notice when it first came out and, despite the recurrent enthusiasm of a few scattered admirers, has had very little attention since. This neglect is of course the consequence of the sheer unintelligibility of the prose poems that make up the little volume. Language is ordinarily regarded as man's chief vehicle of intelligible meaning, and most critics assume without question that any piece of writing which seems utterly incomprehensible is not worth considering as literature.

Nevertheless, some readers continue to call *Tender Buttons* a notable experiment in verbal abstraction, roughly comparable to experiments in abstract painting. According to this view the book can be enjoyed, but only on condition that we renounce the search for either emotional or logical clues to comprehension. This is the position taken by Donald Sutherland. It is useless, he tells us, to work out glosses for the poems in *Tender Buttons:* "It is amusing to invent them and the result may have a certain charm. But it is perfectly idle. Such a procedure puts the original in the position of being a riddle, a rhetorical complication of something rather unremarkable in itself." [1] In other words there is no hidden meaning; whatever meaning is found will be found in the linguistic surface itself.

On first reading, at least, we find much to support this view. *Tender Buttons* contains three sections, "Objects," "Food," and "Rooms." "Objects" comprises a cycle of fifty-

1. *Gertrude Stein,* p. 77.

eight prose poems, most of them very short and each with a title denoting common household furniture, things that might be lying about in a room, articles of clothing, or such personal accessories as umbrellas and eye glasses. "Food" is a cycle of fifty-one pieces on such subjects as meat, eggs, fish, and dairy products, cake, custard, pastry, vegetables, and fruit. The last section, "Rooms," is made up of a single long prose poem of eighty-five paragraphs. These homely titles, however, seem chosen with a deliberate intent to confuse if not to mislead: most of the poems seem not only unrelated in any way to their titles, but equally unrelated to any other intelligible theme.

It must be added at once that if the reader is interested enough to go over these poems with a certain amount of care, he will find himself drawn with a kind of puzzled fascination into more than one rereading. At least I can say that my own perplexity over their possible interpretation has never served to extinguish (it has rather served to feed) my growing pleasure in the reading. One major reason for this is certainly the fact that, placed as they are in odd, fresh, and often amusing contexts, the words themselves soon begin to come alive: it is not so much the living phrase that attracts us as it is the single living word, with all its latent possibilities astir within it.

This liveliness is secured by the technique of jolting words and phrases out of their expected contexts. Yet although in these poems words have been cut away, with great severity, from their customary denotations, one cannot read as if pronouncing an unknown tongue. These are English words Gertrude Stein is playing with, and we are never allowed to forget it: here a phrase condenses meditative wonder or a droll insight; there—and this happens oftenest just as we think we are beginning to get the drift—we find only a delicate parody of sense. Thus flash after flash of meaning is suggested in one phrase after another; but the meanings break against one another, or at times seem to flow into one another, in a seemingly incomprehensible way. The result of this curious procedure is to focus the mind on words. Just what, one asks after some particularly odd juxtaposition, is this word really capable of meaning?

To this extent, then, one has to agree with Sutherland: no accurate gloss is possible for the poems considered separately, because the words in the poems mean just what they do mean, with all their ambiguities. But does *Tender Buttons* "mean" anything as a whole? I must confess that I have always felt that it does and that the fascinating problem is to discover a sustained theme that will relate, somehow, these broken flashes of significance. For Sutherland the apparent chaos of suggestion is merely an aesthetically intense reflection of the chaos in modern culture. He does not believe that *Tender Buttons* is a riddle—and rightly so, in his own terms, since he defines a riddle as a "rhetorical complication of something rather unremarkable in itself."

Yet riddles anciently were more than rhetorical complications.[2] Along with runes and charms, they were "dark sayings" which bore testimony to the magic of the word. The answer to the riddle of the Sphinx, one should recall, was something in itself remarkable. This double connotation is

2. See Lane Cooper, *The Rhetoric of Aristotle* (New York and London: D. Appleton and Company, 1932), pp. 188-189: "Clever riddles do, in general, furnish one with happy metaphors; for metaphor is a kind of enigma, so that obviously a metaphor taken from a good enigma will be good." (I am indebted to Professor William Alfred for this reference.)

singularly appropriate to the strange yet vital writing—when considered as an organic whole—which makes up *Tender Buttons*. For the little book does bear witness to a kind of magic power inherent in words; and beneath its verbal surface the reader can find extraordinary patterns of linguistic relationship. At the same time, I believe, by way of these very relationships, he will discover that the force at work here is psychic in its origin and spiritual in its goal. The pressure that holds the words in place and gives them all their latent power is the mysterious force of a total personality in the process of self-exploration and self-organization. Throughout the whole, indeed, one feels this pressure as a kind of steady effort—exerted against the resistences inherent in the very nature of language—to arrive at, rather than merely to express, some insight of paramount importance.

I believe, in other words, that *Tender Buttons* should be regarded as a mandala, a "magic circle" or enclosure for the unconscious mind, originating in its maker's unconscious but elaborated, with more or less conscious purpose, as an act of self-creation. In this case the mandala is worked out in words. In speaking of the "unconscious" I do not of course intend to revive the hoary accusation that Gertrude Stein produced her work by means of automatic writing. An authentic mandala is not merely an arrangement of symbols from the unconscious—symbols especially vital to the personality that produces them; it is also a highly organized form, presented by means of the dance, painting, or words. It points toward unity, toward the spirit and spiritual perception, for it is designed to unite the conscious intellectual perceptions of its creator (or the one who uses it for meditation) with his unconscious psychic drives and intuitions.

Thus it functions both as a chart, so to speak, of the total self and as an instrument in that self's awakening. In the hands of a disciplined artist, an original mandala may become a creative form, aesthetically significant as well as pleasing, because it incorporates new materials and revealing insights.

One does not ordinarily look at works of art, regardless of their hermetic qualities, with any concept of the mandala in mind. This unfamiliar approach to *Tender Buttons* was forced on me rather late in my studies, and only after a great deal of the book's meaning had begun to untangle as a result of close reading and linguistic analysis. Indeed I was convinced at the outset that Gertrude Stein wrote these poems with conscious purpose and an intellectual design, which would become manifest if one really came to grips with the structure and texture of the separate pieces and the sequence as a whole.

It is true that in her middle period Gertrude Stein propounded many riddles in her enigmatic writings. But she always claimed that her dominant drive was a "pure passion for exactitude"—more specifically, "an intellectual passion for exactitude in the description of inner and outer reality." This drive, indeed, carried her much farther than most of her contemporaries were willing to go into that enterprise shared at its beginning by so many twentieth-century poets: the "destruction of associational emotion in poetry and prose." With these facts in mind, I have attempted in my discussion of *Tender Buttons* to do justice to the presence of a keen, commanding intellect, which Stein certainly had. But I have also assumed that the writer's unconscious mind was exceptionally active—active, I mean, to a degree rarely encountered in purely literary work. First, one frequently discovers a marked overdetermination of meaning—verbal condensation and susceptibility to multiple interpretation—which is often an important sign of unconscious activity. Second, one finds constellations of archetypal symbols (or rather veiled verbal suggestions of these) which indicate that the unconscious at work here is not mechanically betraying itself, as in automatic writing, but is moving toward unified solutions and creative discoveries. This drive toward unity and new vision is the hallmark of Maritain's "spiritual unconscious."

Such considerations eventually suggest the mandala. But an original mandala, as the reader of Jungian psychology knows, is an instrument in the integration and transmutation of the self. It is therefore highly personal in its genesis, although the surprising fact is that mandalas created thousands of years ago are still capable of appealing, intuitively, to the modern mind. Concerning Gertrude Stein's psychic need to create such a structure, it is probable that a good Jungian would explain it as the necessity for a trained and extroverted scientific mind to turn inward and effect a breakthrough to its own buried resources. But this is only the psychological mode of expressing a bit of ancient traditional wisdom. In any case it need not surprise us that, in effecting her breakthrough, this writer (hitherto so labored in her literary realism) should have played as if in parody with the method of catalogue description. Nor is it strange that the finished structure, since her medium is words, should be a form of fascinating linguistic as well as psychological suggestiveness, beneath a surface that in itself can be enjoyed as sheer poetry.

Apparently little is known of the circumstances in which *Tender Buttons* was written. Yet we do know that the pieces it contains were begun in Spain probably in the summer of 1912.[3] We know too that at about this time Gertrude Stein had become desirous of "expressing the rhythm of the visible world," but that she wanted to "describe the inside as seen from the outside" rather than to portray surface appearances. These rather cryptic phrases remind us that she had begun to compose portraits two or three years before—little records in which she described "the rhythm of anybody's personality." Her break with naturalistic fiction paralleled Picasso's change from his "Negro period" to cubism, which started after his visit to Spain in 1908. Also inspired by Spain, *Tender Buttons* reflects Gertrude Stein's transition from fiction to poetry as well as the beginning of the "destruction of associational emotion" in her writing.

Years afterward, Stein referred to the writing of her middle period as painting and spoke of *Tender Buttons* as a series of still lifes. The latter term is particularly suggestive in relation to "Objects," though the poems themselves seem to

3. With regard to the exact date of composition, there seems to be some uncertainty. In the *Yale Catalogue* (p. 45), *Tender Buttons* is listed under the period 1910-1912. In *Gertrude Stein* (p. 69), Sutherland says that "what precipitated the change which led to *Tender Buttons* for Gertrude Stein was a trip to Granada in 1911." According to Elizabeth Sprigge in *Gertrude Stein: Her Life and Work* (New York: Harper and Brothers, 1957; pp. 91, 94), "In the summer of 1912 [Stein] and Miss Toklas went to Spain again . . . Back at the rue de Fleurus she resolved her Spanish inspiration in *Objects Food Rooms,* the series of short often parodied pieces which make up the volume *Tender Buttons.*" In *The Third Rose* (p. 152), Brinnin says: "In the spring of 1912, Gertrude went to Spain with Alice and there began to write a series of stark, lively, and, to the general mind, ineluctably opaque literary exercises that were in many ways the equivalents of the inside-out still lifes of the cubist painters." Hoffman in *The Development of Abstractionism in the Writings of Gertrude Stein* (p. 175) says that "Gertrude Stein wrote *Tender Buttons* in 1913, on one of the trips she and Alice took to Spain."

have little if anything to do with the objects to which the titles refer. For example, "Eye Glasses" reads as follows: "A color in shaving, a saloon is well placed in the centre of an alley." It is possible, however, to find an occasional glimmer of suggestion, as if the concrete object had served as a point of departure for a free fantasia. But the writer returns to this point seldom, and in a very oblique way. It is easy, therefore, to assume that these poems—which do not make clear sense after many readings—are an effort to create in words, as Sutherland suggests, the kind of abstract departure from appearance which was achieved in painting by the cubists.[4]

It is true that Gertrude Stein admired the painter's "innocence of the eye"; she doubtless required a similarly detached perception from the writer. And there is so much allusion in *Tender Buttons* (especially in "Objects") to color, light, vision (or blindness), and the eye that one might seem fully justified in assuming that in these still lifes she is discussing, in a peculiarly garbled and dislocated way, not so much the object as the cubistic vision of the object. Indeed, it is very possible that some such intention prompted her at the outset. At any rate, the allusions in "Objects" to light, visual perception, and the organ of vision form so clear a pattern that the eye (including its evolutionary development) is certainly a main theme in the complex Object of her meditations. In fact, I believe that the eye, both literally and symbolically, is the point of departure for the whole of *Tender Buttons.*

4. The analogy with cubist painting has become the chief point of departure for discussion of Stein's purpose and style in *Tender Buttons.* See also Brinnin, *The Third Rose*, p. 162, and Hoffman, *The Development of Abstractionism*, p. 179.

Nevertheless it is only one theme. Gertrude Stein was thoroughly conscious, in spite of her love of painting and her enthusiasm for the cubists, of the truth that painting and literature cannot perform the same functions. Looking at the paintings of the cubists may well have awakened in her an interest not merely in the "new vision" they expressed, but in the processes by which the "new" comes to birth amid the symbolic forms of civilization. Here what Hegel has to say about the appearance of the new is illuminating. According to him, it appears "at first a whole lying concealed and hidden in bare abstraction," and is therefore unintelligible: "It seems empty to a consciousness filled with the old content with its expansive detail and definitely determined distinctions." [5] But, for Gertrude Stein, the problem was how to empty words of their familiar content in order to fill them with the new vision. Here I believe that theories regarding the origins of speech are relevant—in particular, those of Giambattista Vico, who emphasized the close connection between sensory perceptions and the root ideas of language, noting the pictorial element in Egyptian hieroglyphs and Chinese characters and maintaining that all nations at first pictured reality in their speech.[6]

Now Gertrude Stein was always very fond of Chinese poetry, and two passages in *Tender Buttons* seem to suggest

5. *The Phenomenology of Mind,* trans. J. B. Baillie, 2 vols. (London and New York: S. Sonnenschein and Macmillan Company, 1910), I, 12.

6. *The New Science* (Ithaca: Cornell University Press, 1948), pp. 18-19. In characterizing poetic logic, Vico wrote: "In such a logic, sprung from such a metaphysics, the first poets must have given names to things from the most particular and the most sensible ideas" (p. 117). Though it seems unnecessary to establish a direct link between Stein and Vico, it is of some interest to note that Fausto Nicolino's edition of *Scienza nuova* began to appear in a series of volumes in 1911.

that when she wrote them she was thinking of the composition of the Chinese language out of root ideas.[7] In the first of these passages, she speaks of a "Chinese chair" (p. 64); in the second, she writes "Alike and a Snail, this means Chinamen" (p. 66).[8] If I am right, a "Chinese chair" refers to a Chinese monosyllabic speech form, or a root idea and its pictogram, and "Alike and a snail" describes the Chinese method of extending the meanings of these root ideas and of constructing ideograms to represent them. In other words, I think that Stein made a deliberate effort to revive the root meanings of English words—to recover the pictorial element in them and so attach them again to sensory perception. For primitive root meanings are essentially pictorial, though changes in the forms of the words that carry them have almost completely obscured this fact in English. At any rate, I believe it was in the sense of root meanings as picturing reality that Gertrude Stein described the writing of her middle period as painting.

It may have been out of some such idea, and out of theories of the genesis of both old forms and new content such as

7. In "An Elucidation," the word "china" appears in connection with what I believe to have been Stein's habit of "painting" verbal still lifes in order to induce mental focalization and radiation: "She found china easily adaptable. In using the word china she had in mind porcelain and also painted wood and even painted tin and dishes. She sometimes felt the need of silver and radishes" (12). "Radish," of course, simply means "root." Years later, in "The Portrait of Thornton Wilder," she played upon the word "china" in such a way as again to suggest pictographic writing: "In china china is not china it is an earthenware. In China there is no need of China because in China china is china" (GHA, 36). The passage reminds us that in Chinese "name" and "nature" are related. Implicit also is the knowledge that Chinese is composed of unchanging monosyllabic speech forms, each expressing a root idea, which is represented by a unique scribal symbol.

8. Page references for *Tender Buttons* are to the 1914 Claire Marie edition.

those of Hegel and Vico, that Gertrude Stein began, shortly before she wrote *Tender Buttons,* to reflect very profoundly upon the nature of words, their root meanings, and the impossibility of accounting for the symbolic forms of language either in purely historical or in purely psychological terms. Out of this philosophical interest came the possibility that these strange colorless sounds or written signs might come alive again—if one could only wrench them out of the grooves of habitual use in which they had become slick and meaningless. This reflection was destined to deepen and intensify over twenty-five years of literary labor: Gertrude Stein devoted a great deal more attention to her medium, considered in itself, than writers ordinarily do. A careful linguistic analysis of *Tender Buttons* (with much attention to etymology and primitive word roots) convinces me that the creative source, although not perhaps the temporal beginning, of her long preoccupation is to be found in the discoveries she made while writing these poems. The *word,* then, is parallel to the *eye,* as a twin theme. Along with the power derived from vision, she is thinking of the powers, and developments, of words.

Certainly "Objects," at least, may be read with considerable illumination as a series of free meditations on the eye (or the conditions of vision) and the depths of word meanings, as well as the concrete object selected for contemplation—the same title and the same poem can refer simultaneously to these varied themes. I do not mean that one can always translate the meditations into logical English or convince every reader that there is any "right" reading. Yet without any clue whatever, one finds the words burning themselves into one's attention and stimulating inquiry into their origins and possible meanings. And with the clue of this threefold interpretation, much that otherwise seems arbitrary deepens in suggestive meaning, in spite of an irreducible element of uncertainty.

The theme of color, light, and vision, dominant in "Objects," returns only in a subdued (or rather more veiled and symbolic) form in the succeeding sections. With the aid of Gray's *Anatomy*, however, I have been able to correlate most of the poems in "Objects" with a separate organ or function of the eye, and all of them with some facet of the theme of vision. To present this material here, in a convincing way, would require many pages of detailed and tedious analysis. It may suffice to give only a few examples of this complexity of allusion, which includes frequent references to the embryology of the eye, as well as to color perception, the spectrum, and brightnesses and color mixtures.

The general idea of the development of the eye from the primitive ocular vesicle is introduced in "A Carafe, That Is a Blind Glass," the first piece in the book. "Glazed Glitter" (no. 2, p. 9) seems to describe the cornea; "A substance in a Cushion" (no. 3, p. 9), the chemical structure of the cornea and the sclerotic coat of which it is a part.[9] With "Objects" (no. 25, p. 21) we come to the perception of images, to the action of the lens itself, and to the possibility of three-dimensional perspective. "An Umbrella" (no. 34, p. 22) might well describe the fovea or *macula lutea;* "A Little Bit of a Tumbler" (no. 38, p. 23), its function; "A Waist" (no. 36, p. 23), the ciliary muscle. "A Little Called Pauline" (no. 46, p. 25) is an especially interesting clue to the intention of

9. The pieces in *Tender Buttons* are not numbered; I have added numbers to emphasize sequence.

the whole, since the witty linguistic suggestion in the title certainly seems to convey a reference to the pupil. "Pauline," of course, is the feminine form of "Paul" (L. *paulus*, little). "A Little" refers clearly to a little girl, but equally clearly (when we have caught the idea of Latin derivation) to the pupil of the eye (L. *pupa*, girl; diminutive, *pupilla*, whence not only pupil, a young student, but the pupil of the eye).

These are scattered samplings from a wealth of material, and such wealth need not surprise us. Gertrude Stein was a trained anatomist, thoroughly familiar with embryology as well as comparative anatomy. It seems natural that she should have used this background of knowledge when she began to allude to the eye as a symbol—the immemorial symbol of intellectual vision, concentration, and selfhood.

But as I have already indicated, it is impossible to regard the eye, whether literally or symbolically, as the sole theme of Gertrude Stein's meditations in this work. The writer's medium is language, and the color of words is a very different thing from the color of colors. *Color* derives from the Indo-European root KAL, to cover or hide, and we should remember that words conceal meanings as well as reveal them—and most frequently by way of their ambiguities. Even in her early period, which was devoted to naturalistic fiction, Gertrude Stein had loved the separate individuality and color of words; and part of this appealing color and life was the word's capacity for ambiguity, its power to vibrate with many meanings. In *The Making of Americans* she wrote:

To be using a new word in my writing is to me a very difficult thing. Every word I am ever using in writing has for me very existing being. Using a word I have not yet been using in my writing is to me very difficult and a peculiar feeling. Sometimes I am using a new one, *sometimes I feel new meanings in an old one, sometimes I like one I am very fond of that one one that has many meanings many ways of being used to make different meanings to every one* . . . In writing a word must be for me really an existing thing, it has a place for me as living, this is the way I feel about me writing. (306; italics added)

Stein's feeling for the multiple meanings of words and for the word as a living entity became intensified about 1910. Dissatisfied with the glib and easy use of the mere surfaces of words, the disease that threatens every writer, she began to face the authentic poet's task: the revitalizing of language. This work had to begin, she thought, with the process of renaming, and renaming is the primary function of poetry. But genuine renaming confers upon the object a unique name, expressing a unique emotion. Years later she was to write:

As I said a noun is a name of a thing, and therefore slowly if you feel what is inside that thing you do not call it by the name by which it is known. Everybody knows that by the way they do when they are in love and a writer should always have that intensity of emotion about whatever is the object about which he writes. And therefore I say it again more and more one does not use nouns. (LIA, 210)

And later in the same discussion:

I called them by their names with passion and that made poetry, I did not mean it to make poetry but it did, it made the Tender Buttons, and the Tender Buttons was very good poetry. (LIA, 235)

Here is a forthright statement of the central purpose of

any honest poet—the simplest and most primitive purpose, in fact, of which a poet can be aware. It seems to have nothing to do with complicated meditations on the eye or on words either, for that matter: it is apparently one thing to look at objects with love and "call them by their names with passion," and quite another to turn from the object so loved and named to meditations on the act of perception and the nature of names. But the key word, of course, is "passion," which in a poet is as much a passion for the name as for the object celebrated. If something is regarded with wonder and new eyes, it is worth a clean name, untarnished by sloppy usage.

These are commonplaces to anyone who understands poetry or cares about what happens to the language of the tribe. What is remarkable here, I think, is the sustained and passionate concentration with which Gertrude Stein sought, in *Tender Buttons,* not only to look with new eyes and new love at certain very prosaic household things, but also to find the new and living words with which to express her "intensity of emotion." And whether or not she consciously sought to rename her "objects" with the vibrant word—the word that offers more than one of its possible meanings simultaneously—this is exactly what she often succeeded in doing. Just as the vibrant line for which the cubist Picabia was later to seek "would be dependent upon the emotion of the object which compels the vibration" (ABT, 259), so the vibrant word was to arise from the emotion of the object.

But these references to emotion are somewhat misleading. It is not so much the passion as the concentration on the object (the pure consequence of such a passion) which stirs to unity and creative life the "spiritual unconscious." And what the true poet tries to do—what Gertrude Stein tried with unusual devotion to do—is defined very clearly, with no reference to emotion, by Emerson, speaking with a poet's anger against the corruption of language. "Wise men," he wrote, "pierce this rotten diction and fasten words again to visible things"; this alone is "proper creation." Gertrude Stein herself repeatedly asserted that the power to make words conform to things is what distinguishes the genius from the derivative writer.

Thus in conscious literary purpose *Tender Buttons* belongs in the classic tradition. But it must be noted that Gertrude Stein was about thirty-seven when she began this effort to be a poet-philosopher. Hitherto she had been neither a poet nor a philosopher, but a scientist whose literary method, in spite of a certain plodding originality of tone, was Zolaesque in the extreme. It was necessary, therefore, to purify her vision if she was to purify words and revive them. Fortunately she was keenly intelligent as well as persistent: she soon realized that she had to free herself from bondage to the ready-made habits and acquired learning of half a lifetime.

She may have learned from Bergson that she must redirect her attention in order that it "coincide with something of its own principle." To rid oneself of retrospective vision, however, is no easy task. According to the philosopher of novelty and the intuitive approach, one must mount the incline that matter descends and discover the freedom of the vital current, not by "compounding the old with the old and the same with the same," but by "living in the actual present." In *Creative Evolution* Bergson describes the method: "It needs that, turning back on itself and twisting on itself, the faculty of *seeing* should be made to be one with the act of *willing*—a painful effort which we can make suddenly, doing violence to our nature, but cannot sustain more than a few moments." [10]

There is good reason to believe, from the evidence of *Tender Buttons,* that Gertrude Stein with her characteristic thoroughness attempted to achieve a real union of seeing and willing, in act after act of recollected attention. Her creative purpose, of course, was to revive her own "faculty of seeing," to see the object afresh and also to see the new words that would communicate with exactness the quality of her perception. It is true that much of this is what every poet tries to do. Yet, as we have already learned from Thornton Wilder's introduction to *Four in America,* Gertrude Stein was accustomed in her later years to the rigorous practice of concentration on whatever theme or physical object was presented to her mind—holding her mind still in an effort to reject (or let fall away) every habit-formed association, every secondhand idea, every second-rate solicitation from her own egotism. Not a ferocious exercise of the surface will, but a kind of poised waiting, this act of balance and elimination is the prelude, when successfully maintained, to creative dissociation. At such moments the conscious mind is often surprised by promptings of authentic subliminal inspiration, since the unconscious has been previously trained and brought to creativity by a long discipline of concentration.

But the required concentration, or waiting, is painfully difficult to begin and even more difficult to adhere to. In Gertrude Stein's case, I think, nothing but the crucial experiment of *Tender Buttons* could have provided the incentive

10. *Creative Evolution* (New York: Modern Library, 1944), p. 259.

to begin, and nothing but the memory of its discoveries could have encouraged her to continue so faithfully in later years. Be this as it may, a careful reading of *Tender Buttons* suggests that the "seeing" which Gertrude Stein sought and repeatedly found was an intuitive perception matured almost wholly in her unconscious mind, presented to consciousness in a spontaneous flash.

It is doubtful whether she maintained this high level of inspiration throughout the bulk of her later work. As I have already shown in Chapter Two, however, there is much in her ontological studies and in her reflections on language to indicate that she regarded the moment of dissociation, in the broadest sense, as the decisive moment in the creative process. Philosophically, the chief emphasis of her mature thinking is always on the moment of discontinuity between being and existence—a moment out of which new forms and insights arise. Linguistically, she tends always to associate verbal staleness and formal grammatical patterns with "human nature" (and in her view human nature is invariably practical and enslaved to habit and desire), whereas she associates verbal spontaneity with the moment of detachment and creative vision. I believe that this characteristic constellation of ideas, which suggests a firsthand knowledge of the experience of authentic recollection and dissociation, first came into focus for her as she waited and concentrated in the writing of *Tender Buttons*.

It is because of this base in recollection that the poems in *Tender Buttons* should be of interest to linguistic students and psychologists, as well as to students of poetry. In spite of the researches of Freud and Jung, we still fail to understand the obscure link that certainly exists between the roots of language meaning and unconscious or preconscious mental activity. But from what is well known in more than one tradition about the purgative and unifying effect of genuine contemplation (whether or not obviously religious in motive), we can hazard the following statment. If Gertrude Stein wrote these poems out of an extraordinary state of brooding concentration on the right names for certain objects, we need not expect to find as a result merely a pleasing verbal arabesque abstracted from the great meanings of experience. For the human mind in focus is committed to the search for meaning. Thus if the search for the novel and vibrant word seems in these pieces to exert a centrifugal pressure toward the extreme horizon of the meaningless, there must inevitably be a corresponding vertical penetration (a partly unconscious digging downward) to the very springs of language and intellectual vision.

There is, I think, an unmistakable authenticity in the opening meditation, "A Carafe, That Is a Blind Glass":

A kind in glass and a cousin, a spectacle and nothing strange a single hurt color and an arrangement in a system to pointing. All this and not ordinary, not unordered in not resembling. The difference is spreading.

Beginning quite simply with the actual object she names, we know that a carafe is a glass water bottle, often round-bellied and with a long neck. If it is a "blind" glass this may be because it has a stopper or because the glass is opaque; but it is a "kind" in (of) glass and a "cousin" to ordinary water glasses or eyeglasses. It is also a "spectacle"—notable to look at—and yet familiar enough ("nothing strange"). Perhaps it is a spectacle partly because it is purple in color ("a single hurt color"—the color of bruises) and partly because it can be an aid to vision and is placed at the center of the artist's visual composition ("an arrangement in a system to pointing"). It is "not ordinary" because purple carafes are rare; yet in spite of "not resembling" other glasses, it is "not unordered"—that is, it is one of a kind, or order, of glass.

But what about "The difference is spreading"? This cryptic little sentence is the break in our reading which forces us to pass beyond the simplicity of the object being described. (The simplicity is deceptive; not all of the "Objects" are described so fully and clearly.) In the shock of bafflement, therefore, one is almost forced to stop and ponder, for there is a sudden experience of emptiness. But as the Taoists always knew, emptiness (the vacuum) is the most important spot of all, because the mind has to fill it up. "The difference is spreading" requires that we look again at the carafe, which is both a "blind" glass and one set off by "not resembling" other glasses. And since such a literal "difference" cannot be the difference that is "spreading," we must reconsider the whole passage. Thus we are led next to look at the words themselves—and especially the words "carafe" and "glass" in the title.

The result is illuminating. For *carafe* is not an old word in French: it entered the language in 1642, as a borrowing from Italian *caraffa,* which is derived through the Spanish *garrafa* from the Arabic *gharrāfa,* a drinking vessel (root— *gharafa,* to draw water).[11] This word (itself not attested in

11. For the etymologies in this section (and elsewhere in this book) I have used chiefly Walter W. Skeat's *Etymological Dictionary of the English Language,* 2nd ed. (Oxford: Clarendon Press, 1893). I have used this particular edition because in it the list of roots exhibits most clearly the

ancient Arabic though current today) contains the letters *ghar;* and these letters happen to be identical with the primitive Indo-European root GHAR, meaning to shine, glare, or glow—a root which, via the Teutonic base GLA-S, is the origin of English *glass.* Moreover, when we look again at the word "blind" in the title, we remember that one of its many possible meanings is "concealed."

Etymologically considered, therefore, the title seems to suggest that a carafe is not merely a kind of glass (a "cousin" to a pair of spectacles or an ordinary tumbler). It is also a concealed glass or, rather, it conceals *glass.* For the root GHAR is concealed in the word *glass,* and thus *glass* (or its origin) seems to be concealed in *carafe* by way of the letters *ghar.* But if this apparent connection is real, the relationship is hidden in the remote past, and for two reasons in the present state of our knowledge cannot be scientifically established. We may leave aside for a moment the obvious difficulty involved in the fact that GHAR is an Indo-European root while *gharafa* is an Arabic (Semitic) word. A less obvious objec-

---

network of interrelationships between words that now, owing to vowel and consonantal modifications, appear to have almost no similarity. This network, for example, is blurred in Skeat's fourth edition (1910). For the word *carafe,* however, which is not in the second edition, I have consulted the fourth, as well as Oscar Bloch's *Dictionnaire étymologique de la langue française* (Paris: Press Universitaires de France, 1932) and *The Oxford Dictionary of English Etymology,* ed. C. T. Onions (Oxford: Clarendon Press, 1966). The entries follow. Skeat: "CARAFE, a glass water-bottle. (F.–Span.–Arab.) Modern.–F.–Span. *garrafa,* a cooler, vessel to cool wines in.–Arab. *ghirāf,* draughts of water; Arab. root *gharafa,* to draw water. (So Dozy and Devic; some identify it with *carboy;* see Carboy.)" Bloch: "CARAFE, 1642.–Emprunté de l'italien *caraffa,* probablement dérivé, par l'intermédiaire de l'espangnol *garrafa,* de l'arabe *gharrâf* 'pot à boire,' non attesté dan l'ancien arabe d' Andalousie, mais courant aujourd'hui dans l'Afrique du Nord." Onions: "CARAFE, glass water-bottle. XVIII.–F. *carafe* –It. *caraffa,* prob. (through Sp. *garrafa*)–Arab. *gharrāfa,* f. *gharafa,* draw water. The word has become CEUR."

tion, however, must be dealt with in connection with the root GHAR itself. It leads me into a hypothesis about language, as well as about what Gertrude Stein was up to in *Tender Buttons,* which may seem unduly speculative to some readers. Of course hypotheses justify themselves only in terms of the number of facts they can coherently explain, and this one may or may not explain enough linguistic facts ever to be accepted very widely among philologists. Still, the evidence I have found in the poems suggests to me that Gertrude Stein was playing with this hypothesis as she was writing *Tender Buttons.*

Ignoring the Semitic origin of the word, let us assume for argument's sake that *carafe* is somehow a derivative of GHAR, as the title of "A Carafe"—a blind or concealed glass—at least seems to suggest. The word *glass* is clearly from GHAR, to shine, glare, or glow; and this reference to the effect of fire in the glassmaking process could hardly have influenced the name for a water *container* that was undoubtedly made of stone or skin at the time its name was coined. It is not necessary to suppose, however, that Gertrude Stein is frivolously pointing to an accidental resemblance in spelling. For there is another GHAR root, with the same form but a very different meaning—to seize, hold, or *contain.* It would seem that she is suggesting that the derivatives of GHAR, to shine or glow, are etymological "cousins" of the derivatives of GHAR, to hold or contain.

But if this is really true, the relationship must be due to a common ancestor, *a parent form,* unbelievably remote and not sufficiently understood to be included today in any list of proto-roots. As a matter of fact it is fairly clear that, if Gertrude Stein is suggesting such a thing at all, she must be suggesting that the parent root is GHAR, to seize, hold, or contain—all the other meanings of the form having stemmed from this one. If the reader will consult Skeat, or any other dictionary in which Indo-European roots are listed, he will discover that there are seven different primitive roots regarded by linguistic authorities as having the form GHAR. These seven homonyms have widely different meanings, which are listed here with no regard to priority: (1) to shine, glare, or glow; (2) to rejoice or yearn; (3) to be yellow or green; (4) to yell, groan, or sing; (5) to rub, grind, or smear; (6) to bend or wind about; and (7) to seize, hold, or contain. And if we suppose that one of these (the one meaning *contain*) is the source of all the rest, then the "carafe" of this little poem is a container and concealer indeed, if not in terms of actual linguistic history, then as a very fertile metaphor. As we shall see, several collateral meanings of the GHAR root and their derivatives form the warp, so to speak, of the verbal fabric in *Tender Buttons.*

In still another way the word *carafe* (via *gharafa*) raises the question of remote origins and distant "cousinship." Arabic is a Semitic tongue. Since the word *gharafa* is not known to have been present in ancient Arabic, however, it may have entered Arabic as a borrowing from some Indo-European word now obsolete. There is a still more curious possibility: GHAR may have been present *as a Semitic root* in ancient Semitic words, now lost, from one of which *gharafa* was evolved. It is not fruitful to speculate further, but the word does at least raise certain profound linguistic questions. Can there have been an original language that was the common ancestor of the Semitic and Indo-European families? (This question could not have failed to interest a modern Jewish writer, at home in both traditions.) And is it possible to suppose that beneath the diverse primitive meanings now assigned to the Indo-European root GHAR, there is some unity of origin and meaning? I do not know whether Gertrude Stein understood or accepted the theory that speech had its origin in ritual; but only on this theory does it seem possible to believe in such a proto-root.

As soon as we perceive the possibility of cousinship between these basic words, it is now possible, except for one hiatus to be considered later, to read the passage as a comment on the growth of language from unbelievably ancient root forms. "A spectacle and nothing strange" refers to the extraordinary yet perfectly natural vista opened up to thought when we penetrate to the idea of such linguistic relationships. "An arrangement in a system to pointing" mentions the articulation of language systems for practical uses, since at the beginning language may have developed by means of literal pointing. "All this and not ordinary, not unordered in not resembling" marks the wonder of those real relationships which underlie a multitude of other apparently dissimilar words, in addition to *carafe* and *glass*. These words are "not ordinary" in their possible distant cousinship; yet in spite of "not resembling" they are—whatever their connection—certainly not "unordered." Gertrude Stein seems to have acknowledged at least some relationship here: perhaps consciously, more probably with that unconscious or preconscious intuition which seems to exercise itself with such point and wit in her perception of verbal linkages. "The difference is spreading" therefore may refer to the ramifications of linguistic growth that can produce from the one form GHAR such diverse sounds and meanings as—to take only a few—*eucharist, green, gold, yellow, grow, garden, curtain, yarn, yard,* and *chrism;* the Greek *chli-ein,* to be warm, and *glass, glance, furnace, fornicate.*

There remains, however, "a single hurt color." In the linguistic reading these seem to be the empty words—the hiatus. Taken with "spectacle" they seem to refer to vision itself, and "blind glass" reinforces this impression: *glass* so often refers to something that permits or aids vision that the phrase "blind glass" wears a striking air of paradox. These suggestions lead us to the literal organ of vision, and the following interpretation is possible. The carafe is a blind glass because it is not the real instrument of sight, though it permits and aids sight: it is rather the container of the eye, the eyeball as a whole. The eyeball is thus a "kind in glass and a cousin" by virtue of its function with respect to vision.

In view of the strong suggestion throughout *Tender Buttons* of growth and evolutionary development, it may also be possible to see a reference here not only to the eyeball but to the primitive ocular vesicle, the primitive cell that is beginning to differentiate itself toward sensitivity to light. (But with regard to any single poem in "Objects" I feel very diffident about the precise reference of the "eye" reading, in spite of the correlations I have found. It is the total pattern of suggestion that leads me to assume it.) With the eye in mind, however, "a single hurt color" perhaps refers to the uvea, the posterior pigmented layer of the iris, which is literally purple; and "an arrangement in a system to pointing" may indicate the complexity of the eye structure, which is so organized as to permit focus and selectivity of vision. "All this and not ordinary, not unordered in not resembling," and "The difference is spreading" would on this reading refer

to the miraculous power of vision and to the ordered differentiation of the parts of the eye which cooperate to make
vision possible. These phrases also carry an especially strong
hint of ordered differentiation in the process of evolution.

Several points emerge from our close scrutiny of this
passage. To begin with, we can hardly regard any one of
these readings as the literal one and the others as a metaphorical extension of the literal. Each one taken as a whole
is absolutely literal, though rather cryptic. The writer's
physical eye is present and so are the words that "come,"
just as much as the carafe is. It is true that the "eye" reading
involves a metaphorical use of "carafe" and "glass"—as the
container, so to speak, of the apparatus of vision. But the
description of the object and the discussion of the words
similarly involve a metaphor: the use of "cousin."

These readings are not merely literal and simultaneous,
however. Each one contains what I have called a hiatus—a
recalcitrant phrase that will not be subjected to the reading
as a whole, although it operates as a clue to another interpretation. If one begins, for example, with the "eye" reading,
he will discover the hiatus to be "a spectacle and nothing
strange," which points away to the "object" itself, as familiar
and yet worth looking at.

Now on first thought all this seems incredibly cunning—
much too complex in its contrivance. But this kind of multiple meaning and overdetermination, as I have said, is
precisely what we find whenever the unconscious mind is
active. The activity is probably neurotic—certainly its meaning remains hidden from the subject—whenever one's conscious mental activity is at loggerheads with the unconscious,
in meaning and intention. This happens in most of our

dreams, whether we are neurotic or not; it is also the case in neurotic fantasy, in automatic writing and similar phenomena, and in the Freudian slip of everyday speech. In these cases the unconscious preoccupation asserts itself in some disguised form. Yet there is always a clue—some absurdity in the dream or some oddity in the choice of words—a recalcitrant bit of evidence to show that the surface is not consonant with the depths. There is something almost diabolical in this kind of self-betrayal, as if the unconscious were bent on tripping up or humiliating the conscious ego.

But in certain other cases, although the unconscious is probably even more active, there seems to be consonance and cooperation, not betrayal and dissonance. Wit is a relatively slight manifestation of such creative cooperation: after a momentary descent into the unconscious (a moment of real "dissociation"), the mind emerges triumphant, perfectly conscious of what it is doing but itself surprised, with exactly the word that permits its malice, or some other awkward intention, to find a neat place within a hitherto unwelcoming context. The control of word vibration in poetry is merely, in this sense, a disciplined and serious form of wit. Moreover, in those symbolic literary masterworks which disclose real "levels" of meaning, we find the same phenomenon: the artist's "spiritual unconscious" is at work, supporting and guiding his selection of incidents and development of the action, the names he chooses for his characters, and the very imagery that forms the stylistic texture of the work.

It is interesting to note that although the hiatus—the recalcitrant sign that the unconscious is at work—is never dissonant in creative products, it is nevertheless always present. In wit it is the element of shock, the slight displacement of accent, which attracts attention and causes pleasure. In great symbolic drama or fiction it is usually some incident that is not at first glance formally unified with the rest of the structure. It exerts a kind of pressure, therefore, to force analysis to another level.

No doubt the creators of complex and difficult work would never stay with their labors, were they not rewarded by a continual fresh element of discovery—a continual revelation of other (and sometimes deeper) meanings inherent in what they are in the process of doing. In Gertrude Stein's case, I believe, this recurrent awareness of unconscious guidance must have been accelerated by the very nature of her effort, so unguided by literary precedent. In describing the change that took place in her work and method after *The Making of Americans* (and the abortive *Long Gay Book*), she discusses this process of discovery in terms of the antithesis between accumulated knowledge and the advent of the really new: "And so it was necessary to let come what would happen to come because after all knowledge is what you know but what is happening is inevitably what is happening to come" (LIA, 158). This effort to "let come what would happen to come" was characteristic of Gertrude Stein throughout much of her career, beginning with *Tender Buttons*. There is a good deal of dross in the total product: some apparently aimless punning, much trivial playfulness, and a great deal of seemingly frivolous humor. But there are also many passages in her books which reveal a musical structure and the development of meditated themes—beautiful passages, with a strange quality of depth and suggestion. It is reasonable to conclude that, though she also published her failures, her successes gave her such a sense of revelation that she went on trying, in spite of the failures.

"A Carafe" no doubt was a crucial success for her, since she uses it to open her most revolutionary work—her manifesto to the twentieth century. I have discussed it at such length, however, because in more ways than one it is a tiny cell of the creative process at work in *Tender Buttons*. To begin with, the vibrations in its single words and alternative total readings suggest something of that evolutionary dynamism which lies behind every organism and simple inanimate "object" open to the awareness of modern man. It points not only to the beautiful modern water bottle, the eye that sees it, and the mysterious name that man has given it, but to the primitive origins of all these marvels.

This "arrangement in a system to pointing," however, rests primarily upon a linguistic inspiration. For "A Carafe" accents with unavoidable emphasis the Indo-European root GHAR, inviting close attention, meanwhile, through the idea of cousinship to the fact that the form has more than one primitive meaning. But one basic meaning is unmistakable. The carafe, as we have seen, may be regarded as a metaphor either for the unicellular ancestor of the eye's complexity or for the eyeball itself: thus it becomes the container, in a sense both temporal and nontemporal, for the faculty of vision. And if *carafe* is a real "cousin" of *glass*—if it derives, that is, from GHAR—it must derive from GHAR, to seize, hold, or contain.

The metaphor of the container extends far beyond the opening poem, dominating the intricate verbal and symbolic patterns not only of "Objects" but of *Tender Buttons* as a whole. Although derivatives of all of the collateral GHAR roots seem to radiate significantly throughout the poems, these words are somehow unified and dominated by the central meaning of an "enclosure." Thus we may postulate, behind the seven homonymous "cousins," an archetypal GHAR, to contain or enclose—a root unrecognized, as a parent form, by contemporary scholarship but represented symbolically by the carafe itself.

There is a fertile parallel, if all this is true, between the twin analogies (of eye and word) which are connected by the carafe image. The ancestral form GHAR, for example, may be compared, as a temporal container, to the primitive ocular vesicle out of which the eye evolved. In the reference of this form to an "enclosure," students of anthropology and symbolism will find a further suggestion: that the dynamic originative cell of the speech faculty may be discovered in primitive rituals celebrated in the *temenos,* or magic circle—the taboo enclosure sacred to a god. At the same time, like the developed eyeball (the nontemporal container of the apparatus of vision), this root form GHAR, to contain or enclose, contains the apparatus needed for perception of those structural metaphors which lie at the very root of language. Depth psychologists and students of Jung in particular will also perceive the link implied here between the mandala and a modern writer's authentic or originative use of words. In other words, *carafe* is the container from which Gertrude Stein has evoked *Tender Buttons* as a whole.

In terms of Freudian theory, "A Carafe" manifests the chief modes of unconscious mental activity. In his masterly discussions of wit, dreams, and neurotic symptoms, Freud has defined these characteristic activities as condensation, displacement, and a tendency toward concrete representation that is often (though not always) symbolic in nature. All three modes depend, to a very interesting extent, on ambiguous forms of expression. Concerning the miraculous work of condensation so often effected by the subliminal intelligence, Freud says: "It is really not easy to form an idea of the wealth of trains of unconscious thought stirring for expression in our minds, or to credit the adroitness displayed by the dream-work in killing—so to speak—seven flies at one stroke, like the journeyman tailor in the fairy-tale, by means of its ambiguous modes of expression." [12] Much of the ambiguity at the mind's disposal is obviously linguistic. But the apparently nonlinguistic symbols appearing in dreams, neurotic phenomena, and religious "revelation" are equally capable of multiple interpretation; and when analyzed sufficiently, this susceptibility is seen to depend on language. As Jung puts it, "what an archetypal content is always expressing is first and foremost a figure of speech."

Condensation and concrete imagery are immediately evident in "A Carafe." They appear again and again throughout *Tender Buttons,* not only in scattered passages with their many possible meanings, but in the many-faceted reference of certain focal images and themes. Take, for example, the carafe image itself: it is not only possible to take it as a metaphor for the eyeball (or ocular vesicle) and the fundamental GHAR root, but also as a container for the poetic form of the work itself. In the nature of the case, to be sure, we cannot actually know in what order Gertrude Stein wrote these poems, or with what mixture of deliberate ingenuity and surprised subliminal inspiration. My guess, however, is that "A Carafe" was written first and that the rest of *Tender Buttons* came out of it later, like a jinni out of a bottle: the

12. *The Basic Writings of Sigmund Freud* (New York: Modern Library, 1938), pp. 478-479.

writer's deepened awareness of its latent meanings and germinal possibilities provided (insofar as she could use a conscious plan at all) the design and dominant themes of the entire work. For the similarity between *gharafa* and GHAR (a connection that could not have been found, so far as I know, in any dictionary) seems to have inspired the rest of the poems: at least they form a connected series of meditations unified through word roots and their overlapping meanings—meditations that literally "came" to Gertrude Stein during moments of recollection.

Much of this material finds its place in the structure through the third process Freud discusses: displacement. Here too we find that ambiguity is essential to the technique. As a mechanism involved in the production of neurotic symptoms, displacement operates to attach a buried complex and its emotional tone to some accidentally associated neutral object. Thus in certain childhood phobias a guilty fear of one's father may be irrationally displaced upon some harmless animal but, since there is no real basis for the displacement, the ambiguity (one member of which is repressed anyway) is a purely subjective error. As a "creative" technique, however, where an ambiguity is really possible, displacement is a slight shift of emphasis—calling attention to first one meaning and then another. Freud comments on the genuine ambiguity of "take" in the following trivial example of displacement. Two Jews meet near a bath house. "Have you taken a bath?" asks one. "How is that?" replies the other. "Is one missing?" [13]

It is not difficult to see that displacement functions as a technique throughout *Tender Buttons*. A striking instance is

13. *Ibid.*, pp. 657-658.

the association of *carafe* with *glass,* which at once raises the question of its own validity. What has happened here is that attention to the form GHAR has been displaced, with respect to its root meaning as well as its actual presence, from *glass,* where attention is legitimate, to *carafe,* where it may be mistaken. In other words this pun is justified in sound (if one may speak of "punning" in connection with primitive roots) but not, perhaps, in sense. Yet it is the pun itself which at the same time attracts attention to the root and veils it in primitive obscurity.

Displacement of accent by way of sound, sense, and synonyms plays a great part in *Tender Buttons.* "The difference is spreading," therefore, takes on a further meaning in terms of Gertrude Stein's mode of composition. She actually seems to have engaged in a kind of dispersal of meanings in terms of an ur-root GHAR, which linked together in her mind the seven homonymous roots with their different meanings and simultaneously suggested synonyms derived from other roots, the significance of which she then interlaced with the GHAR words. William Empson was quite right when he said in *Seven Types of Ambiguity* that Stein wrote with the whole weight of the English language behind her. In fact she seems to have written with the weight of all the Indo-European languages behind her.

Gertrude Stein had been a keen and persistent student of the dictionary for many years before she wrote *Tender Buttons.* No doubt in this reading she pored long and often over the root meanings of words, whether in Skeat or some other etymological dictionary. If she was using Skeat, with its list of basic Indo-European roots, the clusters of related words illustrating the derivatives of each root might well have fixed themselves in her memory. There is no reason to suppose that she saw anything unduly interesting in the root form GHAR until she began to ponder what she had already written in "A Carafe." At this point, I believe, she began to see that her subliminal mind—stimulated by sustained concentration on the object and by sustained "waiting" for the vital word—had come to her aid with an intuitive power of synthesis far beyond her normal grasp. There is another possibility, however. M. C. Chassé has put forward the thought that "Mallarmé made a particular study of the root-meanings of words in his Littré, and purified language by restoring to words senses long discarded." [14]

If there is any truth in the theory that language had its origins in the *temenos*—the taboo enclosure—this form GHAR takes on an extraordinary splendor and variegated power of suggestion. The very fact that etymologists list seven "cousins," alike in form but diverse in meaning, argues an extraordinary dynamism in the ancestral root. We begin to suspect that this dynamism is numinous at its source when we consider these seven meanings as a single constellation: each one of them points to some aspect of an ancient ritual.

In GHAR, to shine or glow, for example, there is a possible reference to the sacred fire which, according to anthropologists, was always kindled in a primitive rite. A few of its many derivatives in several Indo-European tongues are as

14. The reference to Chassé appears in a footnote in Robert Gibson, *Modern French Poets in Poetry* (Cambridge: University Press, 1961), p. 157. What Gibson has to say of Mallarmé's refusal to try to invent words seems particularly relevant to Gertrude Stein: "Mallarmé refused to mutilate existing words or to create new ones as Laforgue had done, because he held that words were living things, that their life was sacrosanct . . . [His] solution was simply to use the words of everyday, but in a manner which the ordinary reader could not hope to understand."

follows: Skr. *ghri*, to shine; Gr. *chli-ein*, to be warm, *thermos*, warm; L. *formus*, warm, *fornax*, furnace; *thermometer*, *furnace*, *fornicate*, and (via various Teutonic bases) *glad*, *glass*, *glare*, *glaze*, *glow*, *gloom*, *glib*, *glide*, *gleam*, *glimmer*, *glitter*, *glance*, *glisten*. Along with GHAR, to seize, hold, or contain, this seems to be the oldest and most significant of the seven roots: at least Skeat believes that two of the others were originally identical with it. These branching forms are GHAR, to rejoice or yearn—whence Gr. *charis*, favor, L. *gratus*, pleasing, and *eucharist*, *gratis*, *gratitude*, *grace*, *yearn*; and GHAR, to be yellow or green—whence Skr. *hari*, yellow or green, Gr. *chlōros*, greenish, yellowish, A.S. *growan*, to grow, *grene*, green, *geolo*, yellow, and *grow*, *grass*, *green*, *chrysalis*, *yellow*, *yolk*. The first of these root meanings suggests festal merriment and ritual supplication; the second, vegetative greenness and natural growth, the objects of ritual celebration in early agricultural times.

Less obvious suggestions are found in the following root meanings of GHAR: to yell or sing loudly—whence *nightingale*, *grumble*, *groan*, *greet* (to lament); to rub, grind, or besmear—whence Skr. *ghri*, to sprinkle, A.S. *grindan*, to grind, and *friction*, *grind*, *chrism*, *Christ*; and to bend or wind about—whence Gr. *chordē*, gut, L. *haruspex*, priestly inspector of entrails, and *chord*, *cord*, *gore*, *yarn*. These derived meanings have evolved, with few exceptions, in the direction of the concrete, practical, and secular. But the root meanings themselves convey a real suggestion of the ritual song or chant, the ceremonial use of oil or ochre, and the (perhaps winding) ritual dance.

Last, but perhaps most important, is GHAR, to seize, hold, or contain—whence Skr. *haruna*, hand; Gr. *cheir*, hand, *choros,* a dance in a ring or enclosure, *chortos,* an enclosure; L. *heres,* an heir (taker, receiver), *herctum,* patrimony or family enclosure, *hortus,* a yard, garden; and *chorus, choir, heir, court, yard, curtain* (and *gharrafa?*). In view of the total constellation of GHAR roots, such words as *hortus,* garden, and *choros* (which actually means a circular festive dance and the *place* for such a dance as well) make it difficult to defend any theory of language that constructs numinous or spiritual metaphors out of utilitarian or purely physical "building blocks." For upon reflection we see that *hortus* not only refers to its own root but carries the overtones of GHAR, to be yellow or green; *choros,* in addition to its own derivation, has overtones of rejoice, sing loudly, and bend or wind about. (In her later work, we recall, Gertrude Stein wrote about the "chorus" with lyric intensity.) Such root vibrations indicate the *temenos* as the primal meaning of this root form.

Despite the danger of importing too much peripheral material into literary analysis, our detailed inspection of this wonderful "ritual root" has every justification here. In writing *Tender Buttons* Gertrude Stein herself was performing a kind of ritual, and one that had a double purpose. Consciously, as we have seen, she meant to purify her vision and revitalize language in writing about common household objects and experiences—to "call them by their names," in other words, "with passion." Elsewhere she described this purpose as an attempt to express with exactness the content or substance of experience: "the inside as seen from the outside." But her deeper purpose, one feels, was probably largely unconscious at the outset, although it undoubtedly became clear to her in the course of writing this set of poems.

She was certainly trying not only to be a poet in the accepted sense, but to open up her own depths, to make available her creative potential, to come to terms with her greater "self." And in a sense that need not detain us here, the purpose of all ritual (however primitive) is a similar one: initiation into greater possibilities of experience.

It is therefore of extraordinary interest that the form GHAR, with the full spectrum of its seven root meanings, seems to provide the fundamental pattern for *Tender Buttons*. Whether Gertrude Stein intended it or not, derivatives from those roots—interwoven with their synonyms—spread throughout the book like an intricate design on an oriental carpet. They appear in "Objects" in terms of color and light, singing, and growth; in "Food" in terms of vegetation, friction, yearning, winding, and bending; in "Rooms" in terms of all these meanings, but primarily in connection with the root idea of the container or enclosure. It is in "Rooms," moreover, that we find a sustained discourse, a grave and almost lucid melody, which rises now and then to the level of spiritual meditation.

But if there is so much design here—conscious or unconscious—how can we explain the surface irrationality of *Tender Buttons* or, rather, its impenetrable ambiguity? The uncomfortable plethora of possible interpretations does make the discourse opaque, although single words have extraordinary life and color. One reason for this surface ambiguity, I believe, lies in the object of Gertrude Stein's conscious effort—the expression of "the inside as seen from the outside." The inside of anything is its substance—"content without form," she was fond of saying. But if one sets out to express the content of immediate experience, he will find this substance dissolving into layer after layer of form, like a series of Chinese boxes or the layers of an onion—the form that language itself imposes on the dissolving moment of pure immediacy. It is a highly instructive fact that immediate experience is thus inaccessible to language. In *Tender Buttons,* however, the steam pressure of Gertrude Stein's attention was focused on the substantial: the inside nature of an experience or—it amounts to the same thing— the substance of any direct experience. One is tempted to say that her language was shattered on the paradoxical nature of this effort.

This is only partly true, though. The substance of authentic inward experience is no doubt as inaccessible to language as is the naive immediacy of the subject-object encounter. But if my theory of the composition of *Tender Buttons* is valid, the words that came to Gertrude Stein came with unconscious prompting, but with so mysterious a sense of rightness that she had to set them down (in all their obscure vibration, their many possibilities) while she was concentrating on the substantial. Their obscurity, however, tends to disappear when we read downward, through contemporary words to their root meanings, where a creative synthesis is taking place. Here we find a suggestion that the roots of conscious experience and the roots of language are one in origin, a fact that may explain the dialectical opposition-independency relation we find today between words and experience. We may have good reason to interpret this unity of "origin" genetically. But in terms of life—your life, or mine, or Gertrude Stein's—creative language, like creative experience, is originated only in the substance of an authentic self.

These hints are given to intuition, in terms of the root meanings of words, by symbols and allusions pointing to what language cannot say directly. For in *Tender Buttons,* when the roots of language are reinvigorated by attentive care, living words seem to put forth like green buds in spring. Or perhaps, in their vertical movement upward, their vital gaiety and peace, they are more a living fountain: the "inside as seen from the outside" of Gertrude Stein's poetic self.

Images of budding greenness or a living fountain are woven into the design and meaning of *Tender Buttons.* If the work is a mandala, it is intended, more or less consciously, to portray and to awaken the authentic self of its creator. But the creator here is Gertrude Stein, and this mandala is marked by her characteristic feeling for dynamism and natural growth. Thus it is very natural that, in the writing, one root meaning of GHAR in particular should vie with GHAR, to contain or enclose, for first place in the linguistic pattern. According to the profound yet simple logic of imagination, the root idea of greenness and growth (GHAR, to be yellow or green) becomes a major theme.

One feels the dominion of this idea in the title itself, although of course we have here a marked instance of the use of synonyms derived from other roots. Oxymoronic in its suggestion of something at once soft and hard, "tender buttons" immediately invites attention to the root ideas of the words. *Tender* implies from its etymology something thin or stretched out (from TAN—L. *tendere, tensum,* Gr. *teinein*—to stretch), particularly a tendril, shoot, or sprout. In its extended meanings it suggests such ideas as delicacy, sensitivity, impressionability, immaturity, and succulence.

Buttons derives from O.F. *boton,* a bud, a button, and F. *bouton,* explained by Bracket as "that which pushes out, makes knobs on plants; thence, by analogy, pieces of wood or metal shaped like buds." Closely related in origin to BUT, to beat, push, or drive, the "buttons" are, of course, the hard little knobs or buds themselves, out of which the delicate shoots grow. They suggest the hard surfaces which protect and preserve the new; yet through the root meaning of BUT, one also feels "the force that through the green fuse drives the flower." Since the words in the poems are to be regarded as "tender buttons," an underlying analogy obtains between language and growing plants, with the further implication no doubt that words too have a driving, secret life inside them. There is also a link through *meaning* between "button" and "eye," for eye derives from the source root AC as L. *oculus,* eye or bud, and the eye was originally quite literally a "tender button."

The root ideas in GHAR of yellowness and greenness appear in the color scheme used on the jacket of the first edition, which Gertrude Stein no doubt chose deliberately, for she was in general color-conscious. The bright yellow of the background is like dazzling sunlight—sunflower or chrome yellow—a color of high brilliance. The front is embossed by a circular bit of thin cardboard, banded by a narrow, bright-green border within which, on the grayish yellow center, are printed the author's name and the title with its three subdivisions. The dark green of the border is the color of the green earth, terre-verte (or the color of vegetation produced by the radiant energy of sunlight); also terre-verte are the letters printed in the central sphere. In the center itself the bright yellow of the background has been mingled with the terre-verte of the border to form a gray-green or olive color—a shade of low saturation and low brilliance.

These colors and brightnesses have enough psychological significance to make the jacket a kind of color chart of the contents of *Tender Buttons*. Terre-verte is the color traditionally associated with sensation, while bright yellow is associated with the psychological aspects of color perception. But the degree of brightness in yellow derives from the high amount of pure white mingled with it. Diffused through all the hues perceived by the eye, yet never in itself perceived, white is always to the naked eye yellowish in hue and, as such, is the color of the intuition in color iconography.

Above all, however, one gets the sense of greenness and growth from the vocabulary of *Tender Buttons*, which has a pastoral quality, a ground tone suggesting *As You Like It*, with its rich verbal play and its forest of Arden. Likewise there is the flavor of Spenser's "Shepherd's Calendar," with its songs and competitions. Meadows, Mayday, spring—all are implicit in the root signs of *Tender Buttons:* we feel ourselves out of doors under rain and sun. But these predominant tonalities of the vocabulary are to be caught only as one grasps Gertrude Stein's method of "spreading" both sound and sense—a method resembling the modalities of musical composition in the way in which themes are stated, broken up, developed fragmentarily, presented in interlacing patterns, and finally resolved.

The first noun in this volume, for example, is *carafe;* the very last word is *fountain,* which derives from GHU, to pour, from which is derived, to select only one, L. *futis,* a water vessel. The words of the title, "tender buttons," carry suggestions of young green shoots pushing forth from a protective case; and the last noun but one at the end of "Rooms" is *asparagus,* a word that probably derives from an ancient root meaning shoot or sprout. Such a cluster of meanings, no matter how much it depends on unconscious intuitions and inspiration, cannot be wholly accidental. Indeed, the last sentence of "Rooms" tells us that a great deal of conscious discipline and a delicate control of form have made possible, in *Tender Buttons,* a splendid release of energy and its images. "The care with which there is incredible justice and likeness, all this makes a magnificent asparagus, and also a fountain." From a container to a fountain—such images imply that "water" is moving in these poems, and water is the primal symbol of unconscious renewal and intuitive power. From the "tender buttons" of the title to the "magnificent asparagus" of the close (and surely a tall spray of asparagus is the most beautiful of living fountains), we sense a corresponding movement of the root energies in words.

This movement of energy within a boundary of form (linguistic form, in *Tender Buttons)* reminds us of the mandala—a suggestion communicated visually by the jacket design. The circular emblem recalls many scientific and occult figures both macrocosmic and microcosmic: the earth itself, the spectral band, the zodiac; the human eye, a living cell, a green bud; the navel (which appears at the first period of life as a button or small projection); a target without a visible center; and the magic circle of primitive rituals. Most of all, however, it resembles a mandala, which is usually a formalized circular design—containing or contained by a figure of three, four, or five points of emphasis. These points represent the chief objects of psychic interest for the maker. In the jacket design of *Tender Buttons* the points in question are, of course, words: the title, the author's name, and the subtitles, "Objects," "Food," and "Rooms."

Concerning the psychic function of the mandalas of Eastern or Western religious tradition, as well as their origin in primitive ritual, Jung has this to say, in his commentary on *The Secret of the Golden Flower,* a Chinese book expounding the techniques of yoga:

Mandala means a circle, more especially a magic circle, and this form of symbol is not only to be found all through the East, but also among us; mandalas are amply represented in the Middle Ages . . . Moreover, quite in accord with the Eastern conception, the mandala symbol is not only a means of expression, but works an effect. It reacts upon its maker. Very ancient magical effects are associated with this symbol because it comes originally from the "enclosing circle," the "charmed circle," the magic of which has been preserved in countless folk-customs. The picture has the obvious purpose of drawing a *sulcus primigenius,* a magical furrow, around the centre, the *templum,* or *temenos* (sacred precincts), of the innermost personality, in order to prevent "emanation," or to guard by apotropaeic means, deflections through external influences. Magical practices are nothing but the projections of psychic events, which, in cases like these, exert a counter influence on the soul, and act like a kind of enchantment of one's own personality. That is to say, by means of these concrete performances, the attention, or better said, the interest, is brought back to an inner, sacred domain, which is the source and goal of the soul. This inner domain contains the unity of life and consciousness, which, though once possessed, has been lost, and must now be found again.

The union of these two, life and consciousness, is Tao, whose symbol would be the central white light . . . and the dwelling place of the light is the "quadrant," or the "face," that is, the space between the eyes. By means of these symbols it is intended to make visible the "creative point," or that which has intensity without extension.[15]

These words are extraordinarily interesting in connection with the stylized emblem on the jacket of *Tender Buttons*. Whether Donald Evans and Gertrude Stein thought of all or any of its possible meanings, when they planned the cover, does not matter. The jacket design with its colors indicates, symbolically but accurately, that through language, as through vegetation, drives the secret force of life. It also reinforces the underlying idea of a psychological enclosure where finite and infinite or, rather, life and consciousness can meet. The jacket design itself, however, is not a genuine mandala, but only an abstract hint of one. The real mandala is *Tender Buttons* as a whole. Like T. S. Eliot's "Garlic and sapphires in the mud," which "ascend to summer in the tree," the poems in this volume are designed to make visible the "still point of the turning world."

Jung describes this "point" as the lost unity of life and consciousness, or "that which has intensity without extension." The poems, therefore, are the "concrete performances" by means of which Gertrude Stein held her attention fixed upon her own inner domain. Like an invocation, they serve to summon repeatedly the lightning flash of subliminal intuition—the creative point. But because the poet was consciously aiming at fresh names for simple objects and experiences, her intuitions seem to concern themselves only with the objectivity and transpersonal power of language. Thus for

15. *The Secret of the Golden Flower: A Chinese Book of Life,* trans. Richard Wilhelm, commentary by C. J. Jung (New York: Harcourt, Brace and Company, 1935), pp. 96, 100.

all their elusive gaiety and droll personal flavor, these poems tell us little enough about the personality and experience of Gertrude Stein, and almost nothing about their ostensible subject matter. Read at the appropriate depth, however, they tell us much (as we have seen) about the interior energies of words. And when we take them seriously as a mandala, we find that they also reflect the psychic process or ritual that Jung calls "individuation."

In actual fact, the mandala merely objectifies in symbols the interior psychic process of individuation. This process involves first a certain devaluation of conscious clarity and reason in favor of the dim and hitherto neglected area of unconscious intuitions and feelings, and then a fusion of the conscious and unconscious phases of the psyche in a heightened quality of awareness. In other words, consciousness has here to meet, purify, and come to final terms with the psychic "other"— the stranger within, the alien unconscious aspect of the total self.

Admittedly it seems next to impossible, on dipping into *Tender Buttons,* to see how any of this applies to these poems. Perhaps Gertrude Stein herself did not see it at first— although she must have understood what she was doing by the time she began to write "Rooms." Of course her immediate intention was clear to her: she "stood under" the process, inciting it by the practice of concentrated passivity. But since it is the unconscious mind that initiates and carries through the drama of individuation (although a creative consciousness is needed for a successful outcome), the "curtain" between Gertrude Stein's literary intention and what she was actually doing can only be expected. The important point is that the pattern of individuation, in outline, gives us an explanation for the underlying movement of *Tender Buttons* through "Objects," "Food," and "Rooms."

This progression is suggested by a certain symbolism inherent in these three titles, which progress from vegetal, through animal, to rational (spiritual) functions. But it is greatly reinforced by the linguistic technique. In order to accent the dominant ideas in each section, Gertrude Stein has interwoven into the texture of the language several derivatives of primitive roots. And the themes suggested by this braiding of roots, derivatives, and synonyms turn out to have symbolic relevance to the individuation process. Thus in "Objects" the imagery of light and vision is primary, suggesting an emphasis on the clarity of conscious perception. Similarly "Food," with its hints of heat and transformation, seems to refer obscurely to unconscious processes of digestion and assimilation, both vital and mental. And "Rooms," which persistently accents in many ways the image of the enclosure, offers wave after wave of relatively intelligible although gnomic meditation on certain great themes of integration and the spirit. Uniting the parts, however, is the theme of vision.

Considered as a cycle of poems on the eye, "Objects," for example, is made up of fables of the cornea, the retina, and the iris—little pieces which remind us that the world globes itself in a drop of dew, the crystalline lens of the eye. It is true that most of the fifty-eight poems in "Objects" lack the almost magical degree of coherence and condensation of multiple meanings that one finds in "A Carafe." But once aware of the eye symbolism, we can trace out these short discussions, which are almost always linked, in a kind of inspired double-entendre, with equally cryptic comments on language.

It is not really necessary to decipher these allusions, although one can do so in some detail. We do not need them in order to see that color, light, and the act of seeing are dominant ideas in "Objects." Forty-two of the fifty-eight pieces contain explicit phrases about light or shadow, some reference to a color or combination of colors, or some allusion to "seeing" or the "spectacle" that is seen. Images of light and color, however, are far more frequent than allusions to sight as such. Several of the following color words used in "Objects" appear many times: *color, red, light blue, purple, pink, white, black, green, blue, yellow, mustard, coal color, rose-wood color, rose, grey, black silver, brown, silver, scarlet, dark grey, straw color, gilded,* and *blue green.* Light images are almost equally frequent; even more so, if we assume that *white,* which appears a number of times, refers to light rather than color.

At first glance the variety suggested here does not seem related to any conceivable pattern of linguistic roots: the color words derive from many primitive roots. But in "A Carafe" the opening pun on GHAR plays on its two principal meanings: to enclose or contain and to shine or glow. Since these meanings fuse in the conception of white light (a radiance that contains or encloses, as it were, all colors or possibilities of color), GHAR is once more the source of a difference that is "spreading"—this time a color difference. Thus the verbal texture of "Objects" suggests the dispersal of colors from a central white light. Although *light* itself is used, in one sense or another, only six times or so, *white* is strongly accented with eighteen appearances; and this frequency, especially in connection with the frequency of *color, shine, bright,* and the various color names, is unquestionably designed.

The radiation of color meanings from the root concept of white light is far more obvious, in "Objects," than the extended radiation of GHAR derivatives from the central root form. In other words, the pattern of meaning cuts across and seems to override the pattern of linguistic kinship. (Similarly, in "Rooms," we find dozens of container or enclosure words which certainly do not derive from GHAR.) Nevertheless the counterpoint of color words and GHAR derivatives is repeatedly brought to focus in *yellow,* used seven times in "Objects," and *green,* which makes at least ten appearances. These words naturally have a place in both patterns, since they are GHAR derivatives as well as color words.

Yet although in "Objects" the GHAR derivatives, as such, are not so evident as the color words, it is clear that they too radiate from the central "light." The emphasis on light is strong in the title of the second poem, "Glazed Glitter." Both words derive from GHAR, to shine or glow, and their meaning suggests the utmost brilliance and intensity of light. Almost immediately, however, the melody of this suggestion passes over into the color words, as we have seen. Meanwhile the dispersal of GHAR derivatives is carried out at a deeper and less obvious level, passing from one meaning of the root form to another. "Glazed Glitter," for example, also contains *gratitude,* which comes from GHAR, to rejoice or yearn. In the third poem, "A Substance in a Cushion," the reference to "A sight a whole sight and a little groan grinding" contains in the last two words derivatives from GHAR: *groan,* from GHAR, to yell or sing loudly, and *grinding,* from GHAR, to rub, grind, or besmear. In this same piece we find "The disgrace is not in carelessness," where *disgrace,* from GHAR, to yearn or rejoice, attracts *carelessness,* a word deriving not from one of the GHAR forms but from one very like it—GAR, to call. "A star glide, a single frantic sullenness, a single financial grass greediness," from "A Waist" (no. 36, p. 23), contains *glide,* from GHAR, to shine, and *grass,* from GHAR, to be yellow or green. (*Greediness* derives from GARDH, to strive after or be greedy, a root that overlaps in one of its senses GHAR, to yearn, but is linguistically quite distinct.)

These are not the only examples in "Objects" of GHAR derivatives. In addition to the seventeen instances of *green* and *yellow* and the examples of *gratitude* and *disgrace* noted above, we find several instances of *grace* and *gracious* (GHAR, to rejoice or yearn), and one of *courteous* (GHAR, to seize, hold, or contain). Their importance, however, does not lie in their numbers but in their accented positions, ramifications, and groupings, beginning with "A Carafe." Taken in isolation, each one of the alliterative combinations—"glazed glitter," "groan grinding," "grass greediness"—could be accidental *sound* associations and purely mechanical. But in view of the light-and-color constellation in "Objects," and the importance of greenness and growth and the enclosure throughout the whole work, these odd and apparently meaningless alliterations serve as a challenge to look again, and more deeply, at words and their root meanings. As a result, we come to see the focal importance not only of *green* and *yellow,* but of the originative light toward which all the colors point.

Light is the symbolical equivalent—the very archetype— of consciousness: the nature of consciousness is most clearly expressed by analogies with light. The light in "Objects," however, seems at first to represent a rather passive and completely extroverted awareness. In fact the titles of the fifty-eight poems suggest a passing parade of external perceptions, or possibly a Vanity Fair in which fashions and manners are treated with exceptional gaiety and lightness.

Better still, perhaps, "Objects" presents a pilgrimage—as motley a pilgrimage as ever traveled from Southwark to the shrine of St. Thomas à Becket. If we let the images begin to move a little, we see the red hat of a churchman, the colored hats of the professions, the blue coats of tradesmen, and a lady with an umbrella. There is "a widow in a wise veil" (the iris, or Iris, the messenger), and a time to eat, with a fire at an inn and a table spread and a chair for each of the guests; and even music, for there is a piano in lieu of bagpipes. There are incidents along the way, too—and at the last, as night falls, one is not sure that he has not taken a wrong turning in the dark and wound up on some village green at the foot of a maypole instead of within the cathedral close, for he hears the braying of a donkey and the bark of a dog. And one of the mummers is still in his costume as jack-in-the-green. But we are crystal gazing, we must remember, and it is all a show conjured out of a carafe.

This magical evocation of the many-colored world is exactly what we should expect in "Objects." In this series Gertrude Stein has used the carafe image as a kind of prism to focus her essential theme and then to disperse it into variegated splendor. "A Carafe," as I have noted, fuses the two principal meanings of the form GHAR in order to point to white light as the origin and radiant continuum of all possible color and appearance. In its absolute purity, however, white light is seldom seen in nature—never, in fact, except under carefully controlled conditions. As one of the shortest poems in "Objects" puts it tersely, "A white hunter is nearly crazy." But once the rays of meaning are collected, they are refracted in a brilliant suggestion of the colored spectacle of things.

As a result the form GHAR (more precisely, the full spectrum of its meanings taken as a whole) becomes in "Objects" the verbal equivalent of light and thus, by analogy, of conscious perception of the external world. But light has been, for thousands of years, symbolic of a more inward vision and awareness. For just as all the colors in nature point to an unsplintered unity of white light, so too, according to more than one tradition, the fragmentary character of man's experience points to the possibility of spirit and the experience of an integrated self. This latent capacity for spirit is dormant in the least developed human being; as the Logos it is implicit in and presupposed by every rational act. The constellation of images in "Objects" becomes very interesting when we recall that the fully awakened spirit has been known by such names as *oculus mentis* (eye of the mind), or *synteresis* (self-watching), or the Inner Light.

Considered as the first stage in a process of individuation, the composition of "Objects" constituted for Gertrude Stein a negative labor, but it was also a creative act. Thus two contrary movements are discernible in it: one, a progression from the rudimentary to the highly differentiated, seen in the evolutionary development of the eye; the other, a return to a primitive state, represented by the regression of word meanings toward their roots. The progressive movement may be thought of as representing Stein's recently developed

interest in the external world of appearances, and the regressive movement as a dramatic portrayal of her effort to
revert to a naive state of consciousness. The purpose of the
two movements is, of course, the same: to release the springs
of creativity in a highly differentiated consciousness, hitherto
engaged in the intellectual processes of scientific classification and analysis. Activity of this sort consists essentially of
a *dépouillement*, a stripping away of familiar forms of
thought and habitual language patterns; it involves, for example, ignoring resemblances and avoiding literary references of the kind we find in Joyce's *Ulysses*. As Stein put it,
"I would not know what I knew about everything what I
knew about anything" (LIA, 158). The danger of such
denuding is that, in sheer inner vacuity, the mind will go to
sleep or automatism will rule. But even our dreams, as Freud
has shown, are purposive beyond our conscious will.

There is indication toward the end of "Objects" that Gertrude Stein sought to approach automatism and that she
found it difficult to write anything. For example, in "A
Leave," her perception appears to contract to the narrowest
edge of awareness and, though her attention is not relaxed,
writing seems to be a matter of muscular movement rather
than mental activity. But the voice is the same one we have
been hearing all along: "In the middle of a tiny spot and
nearly bare there is a nice thing to say that wrist is leading.
Wrist is leading" (no. 52, p. 27). "Peeled Pencil, Choke" (no.
56, p. 29) consists of only three monosyllables: "Rub her
coke." Here color has been reduced to a gray monotone and
objects to an undifferentiated mass ("coke"), while there
yet remains the "rub" of bare perception. The title of the next
piece, "It Was Black, Black Took" (no. 57, p. 29), seems to

indicate that she has reached a moment when she can speak only in the past tense of the sensation of black. This poem consists of two sentences, the first of which is held together mainly by alliteration: "Black ink best wheel bale brown." The second sentence, however, reveals the writer's sense of liberation: "Excellent not a hull house, not a pea soup, no bill no care, no precise no past pearl pearl goat." The consciousness that speaks here is characterized by a release from moral responsibility ("not a hull house"—a reference to the social work of Jane Addams?), and its activities, contrary to those of the marketplace ("no bill no care, no precise no past"), are like those by which an oyster produces a pearl or like the capriciousness of a goat.

Thus the last poem, "This Is This Dress, Aider," strikes a willful and triumphant note. If "Aider" refers playfully to Alice Toklas (whom Gertrude Stein's first portrait had described under the name of "Ada"), it also suggests a catalytic agency that assists in the development of the individual in all his particularity and contingency ("This Is This Dress"), here and now, within the frame of the actual world. In its entirety this poem reads:

Aider, why aider why whow, whow stop touch, aider whow, aider stop the muncher, muncher munchers.
A jack in kill her, a jack in, makes a meadowed king, makes a to let.

The "whow" of the first sentence resembles the interjection "wow," which can express surprise or wonder, pleasure or pain; coupled as it is with "stop" it certainly suggests pain. It becomes even more significant, however, when viewed as a telescoping of "who" and "how," thereby reflecting the unity of agent and process. The voice speaking here belongs to a consciousness not only liberated from labor and care, but one that has regressed so far as to risk being consumed in animal activities and given over to automatism ("the muncher, muncher munchers"). But there remains an inner force, a "jack," which with the help of the "aider" prevents the loss of consciousness. The "aider" that raises man above the animal and frees him from automatism is language. As Bergson said, "language furnishes consciousness with an immaterial body in which to incarnate itself and thus exempts it from dwelling exclusively on material bodies, whose flux would soon drag it along and swallow it up." [16] But what of the "jack"?

One need only consult a dictionary to discover the bewildering possibilities of meaning attached to the word *jack*, among which are a flower, a coat of leather, a common fellow, a sailor, a contrivance for turning a spit, a receptacle used in candlemaking, a jackstone, and a lift pump. It appears in Jack Sprat, Jack the Giant Killer, Jack the Ripper, jack-of-all-trades, jack-in-the-box, jack-in-the-pulpit, jack-in-the-green, and jack-o'-lantern. The point I would make is that all of these meanings are actually carried in the fragmentary "A jack in kill her" and "a jack in." Jack the Giant Killer, Jack Sprat, and such toys as jackstones and a jack-in-the-box suggest the naive consciousness of childhood, its play, and its irresponsible carefree fancies—even the subconscious as the psychologist Boris Sidis always pictured it: stupid, credulous, amoral, capable only of association by contiguity ("whow stop touch").

"Makes a meadowed king," however, defines the nature of

16. *Creative Evolution,* p. 288.

this consciousness more accurately. For a "meadowed king" is a jack-in-the-green, "a man or boy enclosed in a framework covered with leaves and boughs, a prominent character in the Mayday games in England." In the naive consciousness there is no barrier between parts of the mind, and this "common fellow," this jack-in-the-box, this jack-of-all-trades, though "meadowed" (concealed in the rites of planting and mowing), is a ruler by virtue of language. Words transform the ruminant animal (muncher) into the celebrant jack-in-the-green.

The phrase "makes a to let" suggests an untenanted apartment, in psychological terms, one without images. If the reader's eye supplies an "i" in "to let," he sees the word *toilet* —that is, a private room for the cleansing and dressing of one's person. With the "i" deleted, there remains only an unoccupied "room." The vacancy fills itself by a kind of attraction and involuntary selectivity. It is this process that forms the contents of "Food," and it is this vacuity, which is really the whole of experience, that must be differentiated afresh in terms of Gertrude Stein's individual vision. Not until "Rooms," where the full range of the GHAR roots is suggested repeatedly in the enclosure passages, are we released from automatism.

Jung tells us that, in the process of individuation, cooking and cooking utensils are all transformation symbols and that the kitchen is the place of creative change. On the surface the key ideas in "Food" are heat and cooking, but the underlying processes suggested by the vocabulary seem to be assimilation (both physiological and psychological) and purification. Invisible and involuntary, these processes go on for the most part in the dark of the unconscious, breaking into consciousness as energy is transformed into light. The GHAR derivatives, therefore, are relatively fewer than in "Objects." I have noted only *yellow, green; gloom, glide, furnace; gracious; curtain, garden, horticulture*. But there are many words that are either synonyms of these derivatives or of other roots that conceal the radical ideas of the GHAR formations. The connection is obvious in *joy*, which overlaps GHAR, to rejoice, whereas it is concealed in *rest* (one of the recurrent words in "Food"). For *rest* stems from RA, to rest, to be delighted, to love (whence also *erotic* and *ram*), and in its equivocal suggestion of a passive activity implies the attractive power of feeling and the beginning of valuation in terms of pleasure and pain. When all goes well during rest, there is rejoicing, or "glowing"—the bodily warmth of generation and desire followed by satiety. Consumed in aggressive action, its harmonies are retrospective—as she says in "Rooms," "the remains of an offering," and its disharmonies result in suffering. Stored in a reservoir, this generative power bursts forth disruptively or glides away along the channels of custom. If warmth is not dissipated, however, but sublimated, it turns into light.

Thus words like *singing, tune, harmony, resonance, scream,* and *glees,* all of which overlap GHAR, to yell or sing loudly, refer to the dissipation of this warmth, as do words like *butter, salve, lard,* and *baste* (to pour fat over meat). In contrast, *mellow* and *mill* (both from MAR, to grind or rub), which overlap GHAR, to rub, grind, or besmear, suggest the sacraments of birth, marriage, and death. Opposed to these words are those referring to the sublimation of warmth —the "shining" words, linked in meaning to GHAR, to glow.

Such words are as conspicuous as *sun* and *Sunday,* but more frequently their light is hidden as in *Tuesday* (DIW, to shine, whence Gr. *Zeus* and E. *jovial), morning* (MAR, to shine), and *string* (STAR, to spread, whence *star,* literally a scatterer of light). The enclosure or container synonyms refer to household or civic economy, and except for *room, shelter, house,* and *kitchen* they are "storage" receptacles, like *prison, jar, sack, bin, cage, chest, trunk,* or small utensils like *pan, cup,* and *spoons.* Even the general term *receptacle* is a diminutive. With these synonyms of GHAR, to seize, grasp, or contain, also belongs *exercise,* which means literally "to drive out of an enclosure" (ARK, to keep, protect, whence *arcana* and *ark).*

One cluster of words, all related in meaning to GHAR, to bend or wind about, are particularly interesting in connection with the processes of assimilation. In this group belong *control* (counter-roll), *ham* (KAM, to be crooked), *mission* (MAT, to whirl, turn, throw, spin), *turn, lean, curve, roll, wheel, volume, curl, bent, winding, worsted* (twisted yarn), and *sausages* (SAR, to flow). It should be recalled that GHAR, to bend, is the root of Gr. *chordē* (gut), L. *haruspex* (inspector of entrails), A.S. *gor* (dirt), and *chord, cord, gore,* and *yarn.* Both *dirt* and *dirty* occur many times in "Food," constellated with other words of bending and winding, in such a way as to suggest the excremental.

In fact, purgation or purification would seem to be the goal of the activity in "Food." If *Tender Buttons* is really hermetic—that is, a work of individuation—then the basic image at this stage is purification by fire. If one thinks of the carafe of "Objects" as a kind of *vas hermeticum,* the activities in "Food" are both chemical and alchemical. Melting, liquefaction, circulation, separation, mixing, coagulation, precipitation, elevation, exaltation, and projection all occur in a retort over fire. As light dominates "Objects," so heat dominates "Food."

These basic ideas of transformation are found in another set of roots that are close in both sound and sense to the GHAR group, and I introduce them because they are the sources of much of the vocabulary of "Food." I refer to the eight KAR forms, which mean to make (whence *autocrat, create, cereal, ceremony, crescent, increase, concrete*); to move, speed, or run (whence *bucolic, pole* [axis, pivot], *monopoly, current, course, celerity, car, carol, garter, garrotte, horse, calash*); to project or stand up (whence *colophon, cervical, cerebrum, culminate, column, hill, holm, haulm*); to hurt or destroy (whence *glaive, gladiator, claymore, harbor, harry, herring*); to be hard or rough (whence *careen, corner, cornet, cancer, canker, horn, hornet, hart, calx, calculate, chalk, sugar*); to curve or roll (whence *crimson, cycle, cylinder, circus, circle, collar, crown, ring*); to burn (whence *ceramic, cremation, carbon, culinary, kiln, hearth*); to cry out, exclaim, or call (whence *calends, council, claim, clear, class, hale, haul*). Of derivatives from these KAR forms, the following appear in "Food": *pole, current, horse; crescent, excellence; culminate, hill; chalk, sugar, corner; circle, collar, ring; claim, clamor* and *excreate* (apparently a coinage from "excrete" and "create").

The link between the GHAR and the KAR roots is explicitly made in "Roastbeef":

Please spice, please no name, place a whole weight, sink into a standard rising, raise a *circle*, choose a right around, make the resonance accounted and gather *green* any *collar*. (pp. 37-38; italics added)

Here *green* (GHAR, to be yellow or green, to glow) is brought into conjunction with *circle* and *collar* (both from KAR, to curve or roll), a meaningless constellation until one looks at the roots and perceives them winding in and out. The strained puns in *collar* (*color* and *choler*), the echoing of idea in *circle* and *around,* and the conjurer's incantation ("raise a circle") accompanied by the making of a circle containing "Jehovah's name, / Forward and backward ana-grammatised" ("choose a right around"), taken together, suggest some kind of effort to raise Demogorgon, but it seems only to refer to the vibrations in words ("make the resonance accounted"). When we discover that the root of *spice* is SPAK, to see, and that of *please* is PARK, to ask or beg, from which *pray* derives, and when we learn that *name* is probably from GNA, to know, while *choose* derives from GUS, to choose or taste (whence *gustatory, gusto*), the words in this sentence begin to interweave like dancers in a ballet. Here is no black magic: the pattern of this dance is an aubade, a morning song of creative activity before sunrise.

The pressure generated in the course of "Food" produces sustained effects in the early pieces, but as it mounts it breaks out intermittently into various absurdities. Increasingly a violent wrenching apart of syllables and even letters occurs, and spelling breaks down, as when *read* is written for *red,* or *reed* for *read.* The separation of syllables is one of the commonest devices, as in "in wit, a rested development" ("End of Summer," no. 22, p. 52). In "a corn a corn yellow and green mass is a gem" ("Lunch," no. 11, p. 48), *acorn* has been separated into two words, while the colors of *corn* (*yellow* and *green*) are distinguished and then the two terms *acorn* and *corn* are united ("mass") in the word *gem* (L. *gemma,* a swelling, bud, gem, jewel). The overdetermination here involves sense more than sound and depends upon visualization for its effect. Though it may not be very meaningful, this passage is more than mere automatism: its tone is playful, not compulsive. It contains no demon, only a bit of verbal legerdemain. In spite of such instances, the intention of "Food" is the attainment of freedom from retrospective vision by temporarily treating words as if they were solids that could be cut up into sections. Yet these outrageous puns, these shards of language, still carry their meanings in their roots, and we are aware of a "mind under" the nonsensical collisions. At the end of "Food" we are told to "Read her with her for less" (p. 59), an indication that the poet's ego has been diminished by submission to the mechanisms of association that go on in the unconscious mind. As a stage in the process of individuation, "Food" represents the differentiation of the self from the "I" that thinks or, better, an enlargement of the self to include more than "I think." Since Gertrude Stein's buried function had been feeling (the opposite of the intellect in Jungian psychology), we may say that she has raised feeling from the unconscious into consciousness—that it is the function "driven out of an enclosure" by the exercise of writing "Food."

In "Rooms," the third section of *Tender Buttons* and also the third stage of individuation, we may expect to find integration at a transpersonal level, and here we find emerging again the references to the eye as *oculus mentis*—references that carry the full spiritual range of the GHAR roots. In "Rooms" the spreading of the root ideas of GHAR takes the form of synonyms rather than derivatives, and the "enclosure" words predominate over the "shining" words. *Room* derives from a Teutonic base RU-MA, meaning a space, originally a place at a table, but now a generic term for any enclosed space. Synonyms for *room* which appear in "Rooms" are *enclosure* and *closet* (from sklu, to shut), *chamber* (kam, to bend), *hall* and *cellar* (kal, to hide or cover, whence also *conceal, occult, cell, color, hull, husk, hole*). These words suggest the *temenos,* the sacred enclosure, and ark, to keep or protect, *(ark, arcana).* (ark is probably by metathesis related to the kar forms). *House* (ku, to cover, the root of *church)* and *building* (of Scandinavian origin) also appear in "Rooms," as do words like *entrance, gate, door,* and *window,* and such place words as *wall, curtain,* and *border;* container words such as *can, canister, stove, sack,* and *package* also appear a number of times.

In connection with the basic idea of enclosure, the words denoting the midpoint are extremely important, for they tie in with the eye imagery of "Objects" and with the "I" references in "Food." Of these words, *centre* and *target* are most significant. *Centre* (from Gr. *kentron,* a goad, spike, prick, center) appears many times throughout *Tender Buttons,* most frequently in "Rooms"; but *target* (from the Teutonic base targa, enclosure, border), which appears only once, is the word that unites the concept of an enclosure with the idea of a central point or goal, and thus leads us back to the eye itself which, spiritualized, may be identified with the "window" (wind-eye) of the soul. The passage in which *target* occurs is placed toward the middle of "Rooms" in a context that needs further exposition, but I shall cite it here, for it focuses the eye-word-self imagery of *Tender Buttons* upon the freedom, timelessness, and clarity of a purified consciousness:

Almost very likely there is no seduction, almost very likely there is no stream, certainly very likely the height is penetrated, certainly certainly the target is cleaned. (p. 70)

In "Food" Gertrude Stein had asked, "What is the custom," and had answered by saying, "the custom is in the centre" (p. 42); as I have shown, it was this custom and this center, the sources of retrospective vision, of time, identity, and causality, from which she was seeking liberation. Therefore in the opening sentence of "Rooms" she gives herself a command: "Act so that there is no use in a centre" (p. 63). Denuded of wont and custom ("use"), the goal of her activity thus becomes, in the words of Bishop Berkeley, "not the light that enlightens, but the source of that light." [17] Objective in its direction but not an effect of force ("seduction"), this activity is not a process in time ("very likely there is no stream") but an elevation ("very likely the height is penetrated")—an ascent toward the One, which Berkeley called the *Fons Deitatis,* the fountainhead or spring out of which creation comes, the *punctum stans* without either temporal or spatial extension, and the realm of ideas, percepts, and the nonself. Individuated in a human consciousness, it is a colorless enclosure, being instead of existence. Gertrude Stein calls it a "plain hill" and implies that it is not contained in the nervous current flowing through the organism:

A plain hill, one is not that which is not white and red and green, a plain hill makes no sunshine, it shows that without a disturber . . . a hill is a hill and no hill is contained in a pink tender descender. (p. 68)

The activity of a consciousness in which this point is

17. "Siris," *The Works of George Berkeley,* ed. A. C. Fraser, 4 vols. (Oxford: Clarendon Press, 1901), III, 289.

reached can only be described as pure potentiality, not a vision but vision itself, the operation of neither the outgoing nor the ingoing will but of both. It is the sort of activity T. S. Eliot prays for in "Ash Wednesday": "Teach us to sit still." But "sitting still" is absolute passivity, the storing up of power that demands expression, and it precedes creativity:

Lying in a conundrum, lying so makes the springs restless, lying so is a reduction, not lying so is arrangeable.

Releasing the oldest auction that is the pleasure some still renewing. (p. 70)

"Releasing the oldest auction" suggests the freedom of creative expression, for *auction* derives from WAG, to be strong, vigorous, or watchful, to wake, whence such words as *vegetable, vigor, vigilant, author, augment, watch,* and *wax* (to grow). The source of a fresh evaluation of experience, it is "the capture of reversible sizing" (p. 75) in the spontaneous perception of the new, the "sensible decision" (p. 78). Now a fresh perception is always the work of an individual consciousness, but its "centre" is no longer the walled enclosure of formulated thought; it is both a *kentron* (a spike or goad) and a target—the arrow and the bull's eye at once. The self is the atmosphere that furnishes the medium for the trajectory of the arrow, being created by, as well as creating, its parabola. The uniqueness of this parabola appears first as distortion, but it has measured a value. This is what Emerson meant when he said that "perception is not whimsical but fatal." And I believe it was what Gertrude Stein meant at the close of "Rooms":

The care with which the rain is wrong and the green is wrong and the white is wrong, the care with which there is a chair and plenty of breathing. The care with which there is incredible justice and likeness, all this makes a magnificent asparagus, and also a fountain.

As I pointed out earlier, the movement in *Tender Buttons* is from a closed container to a gushing fountain, and the word *fountain,* from GHU, to pour, interlaced with images of fertility and growth, comes into focus in the word *asparagus,* the original meaning of which was *sprout.* Here is to be found that unity of life and consciousness which was the goal from the beginning in the eye-word imagery and in the processes of denudation by which the self of Gertrude Stein has become an Emersonian "transparent eyeball."

Reading *Tender Buttons* downward to root meanings has convinced me (and by now, I hope, my readers) that Gertrude Stein was engaged during its composition in the process of individuation, and that the mode of concentration she practiced may legitimately be called a spiritual exercise, though "spirit" refers here simply to the activity of a human mind and has no theological overtones. But this activity partakes of the nature of religious activity, if we consider the possible derivations of the word *religion.* It has been variously derived from L. *relegere* (root RAG, to collect, count, tell, speak), L. *religare* (to bind, root uncertain), and the root RAG, to reck, heed, care for. It would be difficult to say which of these meanings was uppermost in Stein's mind when she correlated writing with prayer. The effort to attain to a state of prayer beyond petition is a form of ascesis, but it has little to do with the vows that "bind fast" or with hair shirts and fasting. It is ritualistic, however, and the radicals of *Tender*

Buttons suggest the vocabulary of religious ritual—always antithetical to the vocabulary of the marketplace.

This workaday vocabulary, comprising words of bargaining, buying and selling, and exchanging, is transformed at the end of "Rooms" where the idea of religious activity becomes explicit in the fifty-fourth paragraph, beginning "A religion, almost a religion, any religion, a quintal in religion" (p. 73). The unfamiliar word *quintal* here furnishes us a key to unlock the hermetic operation of *Tender Buttons,* for it names an ancient Egyptian measure of weight, a *kantar,* meaning "pertaining to the fifth"—a word of Arabic origin, like *carafe* —and in context refers to the quintessential element, that invisible fire worshiped by the ancient Chaldeans and Egyptians as the principle of creativity. This quintessence is the source of Authority, Light, and Life in macrocosm and microcosm, and all religions express it. Prepared for by the radiation of the GHAR forms, the forms of religious ritual emerge in *Tender Buttons* in such words as *cloister, sacrifice, sermon, church, kneeling, praying, righteous, Catholic,* and *Sunday,* but praying is the act of individual participation. It may have been this act of participation in the *logos* that Gertrude Stein referred to in the passage quoted earlier from "An Elucidation." If I understand her use of the term *prayer,* it always signifies unself-centered creative activity. Thus, as I have said elsewhere, although she was not religious in any of the commonly accepted meanings of the term, in Whitehead's sense ("religion is what the individual does with his own solitariness") she was religious. Similarly her writing, viewed in Whitehead's terms ("expression is the one fundamental sacrament"), can be called a religious ritual.

To some it may appear that the "plain hill" has labored

and brought forth a mouse in *Tender Buttons,* rather than a work of either religion or art. Perhaps one must be willing to believe that the activity is more important than the result in order to appreciate Gertrude Stein's efforts in these poems. There is a description in Forster's *Passage to India* that is relevant here. Professor Narayan Godbole, a Brahmin, is participating in ceremonies celebrating the birth of Krishna. To the rhythmic clashing of cymbals, the celebrants sing:

They loved all men, the whole universe, and scraps of their past, tiny splinters of detail, emerged for a moment to melt into the universal warmth. Thus Godbole, though she was not important to him, remembered an old woman he had met in Chandrapore days. Chance brought her into his mind while it was in this heated state, he did not select her, she happened to occur among the throng of soliciting images, a tiny splinter, and he impelled her by his spiritual force to that place where completeness can be found. Completeness, not reconstruction. His senses grew thinner, he remembered a wasp seen he forgot where, perhaps on a stone. He loved the wasp equally, he impelled it likewise, he was imitating God. And the stone where the wasp clung— could he . . . no, he could not, he had been wrong to attempt the stone, logic and conscious effort had seduced, he came back to the strip of red carpet and discovered that he was dancing upon it.

Of no practical value, the old woman and the wasp are the products of Godbole's participation in an effort of the human spirit to "ravish the unknown, flinging down science and history, yes, beauty herself." After the birth of Krishna come the games to amuse the infant God: "By sacrificing good taste, this worship achieved what Christianity has shirked: the inclusion of merriment." [18]

18. E. M. Forster, *A Passage to India* (New York: Harcourt, Brace and Company, 1924), pp. 286, 288, 289.

The spiritual force by which Godbole impels the two "soliciting images," the sense of a completeness that is not reconstruction, the thinning of the senses, and the final seduction by logic and conscious effort seem to me to parallel the activity of Gertrude Stein in the writing of *Tender Buttons*. There is even the sacrifice of good taste and the inclusion of merriment. This point is crucial: it is the merriment and the sacrifice of taste that raise some doubt about those terms "spiritual exercises" and "secular saintliness," particularly for Americans. I cannot refrain from noting that in "secular saintliness" Donald Sutherland hit upon the right phrase to describe both the personality and the writing of Gertrude Stein, for *secular* derives from sa, to sow, strew, scatter. Just as her vocabulary was seminal, so the impact of her personality was creative; it awakened in others, or intensified, their own creativity.

This power to radiate must be ascribed, I believe, to a certain kind of dissociation, or, in Jungian terms, differentiation, followed by integration. In the Western tradition, the Catholic mystic Hugh of St. Victor, seeking to characterize a mental state both void of egotism and highly conscious, spoke of the *oculus mentis:*

Thou hast . . . an Eye within thee, far more piercing than thy outer eye, an Eye that beholds at once the past, the present, and the future; which diffuses through all things the brightness of its vision; which penetrates what is hidden, investigates what is impalpable; which needs no foreign light wherewith to see, but gazes with a light of its own, peculiar to itself.[19]

In *De signatura rerum,* Jacob Boehme, the Protestant mystic, untutored except by intensive contemplation and a little

19. Quoted in Rufus Jones, *The Luminous Trail* (New York: Macmillan Company, 1947), p. 59.

religious reading, also associated a heightened state of consciousness with the eye, and Jung notes that he found among Boehme's writings a drawing labeled the "philosophical eye," used probably as an instrument of meditation. According to Howard Brinton, Boehme associated the visual sense with love and the auditory sense with the "form" of love; thus he linked "sound" (the word) with the expression of love, sound representing the "outgoing will" and love (vision) the "ingoing will." It is worth noting that in the enumeration of the "forms," Boehme's *fifth* form was called Venus, "the beginning of all corporality, viz. of the water, which arises in the desire of Jupiter and Mars." Boehme was a visionary, of course, and his writings are obscure, but it seems clear that by associating *love* with *vision* and *sound* with the *word,* he was seeking to express the aesthetic experience. Attempting to characterize the Absolute, Boehme used language that ties in beautifully with Gertrude Stein's eye imagery: "[The Absolute] comprehends itself in an eye or general longing to a self-observation and perception." [20] In "Finally George, a Vocabulary," Stein wrote: "Writing may be made between the ear and the eye and the ear and the eye will be well and the ear will be well" (HTW, 277).

In *The Secret of the Golden Flower* we are told: "In the midst of primal becoming, the radiance of the Light (Yang Kuang) is the determining thing. In the physical world it is the sun; in man the eye," and "Keeping the thought of the space between the two eyes allows the Light to penetrate." Anticipating the student's difficulties in concentrating prop-

20. Quoted in Howard Brinton, *The Mystic Will* (New York: Macmillan Company, 1930), p. 182.

erly and the dangers of seduction by logic and conscious effort, the author writes:

Should a man have no images in his mind? One cannot be without images. Should one not breathe? One cannot do without breathing. The best way is to make a cure out of the illness. Since heart and breath are mutually dependent, the circulation of the Light must be united with the rhythm of breathing. For this, Light of the ear is above all necessary. There is a Light of the eye and a Light of the ear. The Light of the eye is the united Light of the sun and moon outside. The Light of the ear is the united seed of sun and moon within. The seed is also the Light in crystallized form. Both have the same origin and are different only in name. Therefore, understanding (ear) and clarity (eye) are one and the same effective Light.[21]

Jung's commentary on this treatise describes the kind of ascesis called for here as "the deracination of consciousness," and he makes it clear that the seeker after the Light actually focused upon a drawing of the golden flower, just as Boehme must have concentrated upon his "philosophical eye." Both drawings are mandalas, magic circles. Though no one so far as I know has ever said that Gertrude Stein made use of such drawings, the device stamped on the covers of some of her books may have functioned as a mandala. She makes Alice B. Toklas say in the *Autobiography:* "Speaking of the device of rose is a rose is a rose is a rose, it was I who found it in one of Gertrude Stein's manuscripts and insisted upon putting it as a device on the letter paper, on the table linen and anywhere that she would permit that I put it" (169). No date is mentioned here, but the ideogram must have been

21. *The Secret of the Golden Flower,* pp. 34, 40, 44-45.

discovered about the time Gertrude Stein turned from fiction to poetry, and my guess is that it was actually used as an instrument in the practice of the meditations in *Tender Buttons.*

The empty center of this figure, containing the words "rose is a rose is a rose is a rose," suggests to me the emptiness which the Taoists regarded as the inner, sacred domain. The boundary of words delimits a consciousness becoming concrete in its moment-by-moment experience of immediacy— consciousness and life are unified. It is both temporal and nontemporal, and it contains mathematical succession as well as geometric form, though there is no "progressing." This little hieroglyph thus becomes a symbol of our common experience in which finite and infinite constantly meet, and the tautological proposition forming the ring becomes a *sulcus primigenius,* a magic furrow, generated by and generating an individual consciousness.

May it not be that for Gertrude Stein the activity of writing is the ritual of deracinating one's own consciousness, and that it is therefore a phenomenon of more than passing significance? May not the impulse toward abstraction in the arts of our time be tied in with the need for creating mandalas? If so, this tells us something about personality needs in the present era—something we already know, perhaps, though it offends our science and our reason. Certainly the feeling of emptiness engendered by much abstract art is not entirely unrelated to the general problems confronting the twentieth-century psyche. This emptiness must reflect an inward condition. Like the abstract paintings it resembles, *Tender Buttons* remains vacuous even when it is no longer opaque. Despite so intense an effort as moved Gertrude

Stein to write it—despite its linguistic and psychological interest—this book is closed to the imagination except as we see *through* (and beyond) it.

There is something poignant in the disparity between the depth of insight and the surface flatness not only of *Tender Buttons* but of nearly all of Gertrude Stein's work. This very quality may also serve to illuminate much that is flat and trivial in contemporary art and life. Gertrude Stein saw beneath this flatness. And like another poet of the New England tradition (in which Gertrude Stein must stand), she had to overcome her fears of both depth and height by confronting her own soul. It was Robert Frost who said,

> They cannot scare me with their empty spaces
> Between stars—on stars where no human race is.
> I have it in me so much nearer home
> To scare myself with my own desert places.[22]

22. From "Desert Places," *Complete Poems of Robert Frost* (New York: Holt, Rinehart and Winston, 1949), p. 386; copyright 1936 by Robert Frost, copyright 1964 by Lesley Frost Ballantine; reprinted by permission.

> *The modern man abhors dogmatic postulates taken on faith and the religions based upon them. He holds them valid only in so far as their knowledge-content seems to accord with his own experience of the deeps of psychic life. He wants to know—to experience for himself.*
>
> —Carl Jung

IV. AN AMERICAN VERSION OF THE FAUST LEGEND

Although the trail that leads from *Tender Buttons* to *Doctor Faustus Lights the Lights* a quarter of a century later is a hidden one, there is a unity to them—the unity of Gertrude Stein's lifelong preoccupation with the process of individuation. *Tender Buttons* conceals its goal and method (perhaps only half consciously) beneath a surface of unintelligible charm. It is hermetic and vital, however, as we have seen, because it shows Gertrude Stein in the process of excited self-creation as she searches for the living word. In contrast, *Doctor Faustus* has for its actual subject matter not the voluntary ascesis of the artist (the secular saint), but the self-division of an alienated representative of contemporary civilization. In each work, nonetheless, she has suggested the archetypes of transformation, vision, and attainment.

The Faust story has long been understood as a singularly proper symbol for the history of European man after the Renaissance—so much so, indeed, that although its origins lie in fact and superstitious legend, it has grown into a genuine myth, perhaps the only one the modern West has produced. "Faustian man," "Faustian civilization"—these phrases are everywhere read as referring to a spirit peculiarly aware of time and history, and ruled by that soaring hubris —that thirst for the infinite in terms of earthly power and secular knowledge—which has no doubt produced the triumphs and impending disasters of science and the modern state.

So interpreted, there seems to be little reason for an American writer to present this myth again in modern dress. There is nothing specifically American about the present debacle (in spite of European accusations to the contrary), although it may be true that every destructive tendency in twentieth-century mechanized civilization is accelerated in the fabulously rich country of Ford, Edison, and the Wright brothers. But when Gertrude Stein undertook to rewrite the Faust story as an opera libretto, she was less concerned with the crisis in Western society than with the perennial psychological significance, for the individual, of the traditional image of an alchemist haunted by Mephisto. In this regard her *Doctor Faustus Lights the Lights* seems closer to Goethe's interpretation of the legend than to Marlowe's.

Psychologically regarded, the Faust figure seems to be civilized man, haunted by his own dark other self—his "enemy within"—which Jung has called the Shadow. In this sense the Faust legend may be understood as a monodrama symbolizing a neurotic crisis of self-division and self-confrontation. Although in real life a crisis of this nature may be uncomfortably and unfortunately like schizophrenia, Jung regards the experience as a challenge and stimulus to the process of self-creation and reintegration. Yet he has written so voluminously about the symbolic stages of neurotic crisis itself that it is possible to overlook two important facts: that the true goal of the process—which may never be reached or understood—is self-realization or individuation; and that the method of reaching that goal—whether the subject is passively neurotic or sanely and rigorously self-disciplined—is always one of introverted waiting and concentrated attention. These were Stein's concerns as well, and her Faust libretto is a symbolic story demanding interpretation in terms of the inner conflicts of the modern mind.

She gives us the Faust story, however, with a peculiarly American twist. She does this, to be sure, in a different sense and to a far less noticeable degree than did Mann, in German terms, in his *Doctor Faustus*. There is nothing American in the symbols she uses or in the setting of the action—which is the world of dreams; and the light, flat tone and banal style of the dialogue belong to neither Europe nor America, but to the country of Gertrude Stein's own highly individual mind. Nevertheless, as we shall see, she speaks to the American condition in a special way. Regardless of whether or not her opera is good (or ought to be mentioned in the august company of certain great works on the same theme), the reader will discover that she has presented a "landscape" picturing a spiritual conflict, and that her resolution of this conflict has an unexpectedly close relation to an authentic American tradition.

Perhaps I can best define this tradition by reference to three of its greatest prophets. It was true of Emerson, Thoreau, and Whitman alike that they sought to bring into the consciousness of their time something they felt deeply as the American possibility, or as the purpose of the American adventure. This possibility was not European at all, even though it drew part of its inspiration from Renaissance individualism as well as from the Christian-democratic heritage. For in spite of their emphasis on sturdy self-reliance and the potential greatness of the individual human being, these three idealists sought rather a *fusion* of European individualism with the more ancient view of man's nature recorded in the Vedas and Upanishads—a tradition that found its highest value not in the accidents of personality but in the impersonal Atman (divine Self) asleep in every man. Something in the openness of the American situation and the inchoate state of American culture seems to have kindled in all three sages the hope that here, at last, the common man might have room to reach spiritual maturity and find his true greatness in the cosmic scheme. Thus they gave democracy a metaphysical foundation by requiring every individual to discover the infinite One in himself.

It is not generally recognized, I think, that in certain fundamental respects Gertrude Stein belongs in the main line of this Oriental-American tradition. As a writer, she belongs with the three mentioned above in her reliance on immediate inspiration and in her recurrent emphasis on content rather than form. As a thinker, she belongs with them in her belief that America is destined to produce a new orientation of consciousness which can unite the mainstreams of Oriental and Occidental spirituality. But she seems to have conceived of the problem of the undiscovered eternal Self in psychological rather than metaphysical terms. Because of this psychological orientation, therefore, it is not by chance that her *Doctor Faustus Lights the Lights* reminds us of Jung's theories of the human psyche and its inner dynamics. In his own way, as a psychologist deeply conscious of modern man's alienation from authentic selfhood, Jung has had much to say about the potential Self in man and man's need to awaken it. Aware of the symptomatic significance of such superficial phenomena as theosophy and interest in the occult, he has also had much to say about what the East can really teach the West, if its wisdom is properly understood. Thinking in broadly European terms, Jung does not of course expect American culture as such to produce this desirable interpenetration.

Jung's ideas on literature also have bearing on the forbidding aspect of Gertrude Stein's play, which is difficult to take seriously, or to understand appropriately, because of the oddity and apparent inanity of the style. Jung says that the masterpieces of literature cannot be clear to the society in which they are created because they arise from subterranean psychic currents. They do not merely illuminate the contents of consciousness but, when they first appear, transcend the bounds of intelligibility. The creative artist "speaks with the voice of thousands and ten thousands, foretelling changes in the conscious outlook of his time." In other words, the poet is the vehicle for the unconscious experiences of his epoch: existential actuality reaches the common consciousness through his vision.

He has done the best that in him lies in giving it form, and he must leave the interpretation to others and to the future. A great work of art is like a dream; for all its apparent obviousness it does not explain itself and is never unequivocal. A dream never says: "You ought," or: "This is the truth." It presents an image in much the same way as nature allows a plant to grow, and we must draw our own conclusions.[1]

Doctor Faustus Lights the Lights is probably not a masterpiece, but I believe that in it Gertrude Stein was getting down to something basic in speaking to and for our epoch. The "image" it presents condenses a very significant thought now haunting the collective mind of the West. Some aspects of this idea are thinned out and distorted by popular theosophy; others, by various cults of "authentic selfhood" based on the more sensational writings of the existentialists. From a rather different angle the ecstatic LSD breakthrough envisioned by Timothy Leary and his followers has affinities

1. C. J. Jung, *Modern Man in Search of a Soul*, trans. C. F. Baynes (New York: Harcourt, Brace and Company, 1933), pp. 192, 198.

with this thought; and a vague yet passionate aspiration toward the same goal of heightened awareness seems to impel such gurus and poets as Allen Ginsberg. But it is a thought which, in its serious depth and range, some of the greater psychologists and thinkers of our time are laboring to bring to wider consciousness. In this chapter we shall explore this idea as it is embodied in Gertrude Stein's *Doctor Faustus*.[2]

The Faustus libretto is written in the repetitive, rhyming style and with the flat emotional tone that one has come to associate with Gertrude Stein's compositions in general. Yet it is more conventional in form than her earlier plays: it has none of the nonsequential numbering of scenes or the annoying dislocations of parts of speech so characteristic of the writings of her middle period. Composed in 1938, it is a product of her mature years and belongs to the period immediately following her American tour, when she was concerned with such ideas as identity, memory, and eternity. Between 1934 and 1938 she wrote *What Are Masterpieces, The Geographical History of America, Everybody's Autobiography*, and a number of short pieces on the theme of identity. To this period also belong her novel *Ida*, based upon the romance of Edward VIII and Mrs. Simpson; the

2. *Doctor Faustus Lights the Lights*, in *Last Operas and Plays* (New York: Rinehart and Company, 1949). In the introduction, Carl Van Vechten tells us that the first act was completed by May 10 and the opera completed by June 20, 1938. He also says that Gertrude Stein had hoped to have music composed for it by Gerald Berners and to have a popular edition of the text published by Bennett Cerf. These plans did not materialize: Berners wrote that he was unable to compose anything at the time, and "Early in the fall of 1938, Bennett Cerf informed me that he had written Gertrude that he would not publish the text of the opera. This is the first time then that it has seen the light of print" (p. xviii).

critical essay *Picasso;* and a child's story, *The World Is Round.*

Against this constellation of titles, *Doctor Faustus Lights the Lights* stands out because it deals with a well-known legend. Thus it not only invites comparison with other poetic interpretations of the tale, but announces what is only implicit in the other titles—that Gertrude Stein had emerged from the apparent solipsism of her middle period and was seeking a balance between her own personal vision and the insights of poets of the past. She had started her career with *Three Lives* and *The Making of Americans,* psychological fiction grounded in her own experience. Then she had withdrawn from such realities in an effort to penetrate more deeply into experience and had disappeared into subterranean currents, from which she began to emerge around 1932 (*The Autobiography of Alice B. Toklas*). After the American tour of 1934, the wheel came full circle: she turned outward again to the world.

As I have just said, Stein was much preoccupied with ideas of identity, memory, and eternity after 1935—in other words, she was engaged in the search for a world view which would reconcile the contradiction between finite and infinite in man, a contradiction actually resolved in the individual life and in the achievements of culture. The latter are not the work of memory in the usual sense, but resemble the unconscious memory of nature, in which order consists of the reciprocal realization of the particular and the universal. The paradoxes of being and nonbeing, of the one and the many, of the whole and the parts, lie at the core of Goethe's *Faust;* and it seems appropriate that Gertrude Stein should have built her reinterpretation of the Faust legend on the ambiguity of experience and man's dual role of redeemer and destroyer. The paradoxes of the Faustian dilemma are still very much alive today.

Gertrude Stein's continuation of the legend begins with a Faust who has been draining swamps and applying scientific knowledge to every branch of human activity for a hundred years, but who has suddenly lost his faith in progress and enlightenment. He has invented the electric light and, since he understands the principles of natural science, knows that he has by no means exhausted the field of technology; but the joy of discovery is gone. Furthermore, the world does not really need new gadgets. In fact, there is no use in doing anything. Life has no purpose, for the cosmos is only a mechanism—and man, in spite of his intellect, a puppet. Faust's devil is therefore the same old Mephisto who appeared to Goethe's Faust. But though Stein employs many of the same symbols and events, her hero moves along a different pathway to the reconciliation of the "opposites," the two souls contending in his breast. Her conception of the problem is not directly known to us, but she did drop a hint or two.

In the spring of 1938, when she was working on the Faust libretto, she wrote to Carl Van Vechten: "The theology and the drama I hope will be to your liking." Later she wrote again: "I have been struggling with this problem of dramatic narrative and in that I think I have got it." [3] If the reference to theology means that her intention was to convey an idea of deity, then *Doctor Faustus* is a religious drama, and the problem of dramatic narrative was how to portray on the stage the most abstract of man's ideas. Since one of her

3. *Last Operas and Plays,* p. xvii.

major efforts had been to redesign language in order to free
it from traditional symbolisms, one can be certain that the
stereotypes of dogma and ritual will be displaced by uncon-
ventional objects and action, just as they were eleven years
earlier in *Four Saints in Three Acts*. In this opera she had
wanted to express the internal state of the religious mystic—
what she called "the sentiment of doing nothing" (the Chinese concept of not-doing as opposed to willed activity). In
order that there be something to "see" and "hear" which
would not evoke conditioned responses, she had relied heavily upon grammatical dislocations, setting, ballet, and music,
and had introduced such episodes as the nuns playing cro-
quet. The internal dynamics of *Doctor Faustus* reveals a
similar kind of symbolic action, which draws upon Goethe's
Faust in a general way. But its relevance to modern psychology, Jung especially, is more striking and significant.

The difficulties of establishing influence are always great,
and there is little direct evidence that Jung influenced Gertrude Stein. His theories, however, were part of the public
domain during the twenties and thirties, particularly among
Paris intellectuals, and Gertrude Stein was a trained psychologist. She may well have read such works of his as *Psychology of the Unconscious* (translated 1921), *Psychological
Types* (translated 1923), *Two Essays in Analytical Psychology* (translated 1928), and *Contributions to Analytical Psychology* (translated 1928). She was closely associated with
the *Transition* group at the time that Eugene Jolas translated
and published Jung's "Psychologie und Dichtung" (1930).

Most suggestive of all is the fact that the libretto of *Doctor
Faustus* was composed in the late spring of 1938, only two or
three months after Yale's publication of Jung's *Psychology*

and Religion. Not only does her own reference to theology point toward a similar theme, but both the action and the dramatis personae of the work are unmistakably Jungian. Jung's frequent references to Goethe's *Faust*—in connection with his theories of the transforming function of the archetypes of the collective unconscious—may even have influenced Gertrude Stein's choice of subject. It is equally possible, however, that she simply happened to see in the Faust material what Jung also saw.

In any case, Jung's terminology is almost indispensable to an adequate interpretation of *Doctor Faustus.* On several occasions in the preceding chapter I have recalled what is perhaps central to Jung's theory of individuation: the significance of the mandala as a mystic or yogic instrument of meditation and concentration for spiritual development. But in the discussion of *Tender Buttons* as Gertrude Stein's self-created and self-creating mandala, there was no reason to give the Jungian terms for the stages of that inner process to which Jung has devoted so many books and essays of explication. With *Doctor Faustus* the situation is different. Here we come to a work that puts on the stage specifically Jungian concepts, and, at the risk of going over already familiar ground, it seems advisable to recall them clearly at this point.

According to Jung, the psyche is a unity that comprehends the whole of the indefinable and enigmatic oneness of the living being. It is "immediacy itself," and because "we ourselves are psyches" its facts are difficult to ascertain. Jung defines the psyche in terms of its processes, conscious and unconscious, individual and collective. Its primal energy is libido, the undifferentiated or primitive life impulse, conceived as an intensity of value rather than as a force. Of its two parts, the conscious psyche with the ego as its center is much the smaller. The unconscious psyche, which strictly speaking has no known center and no definable boundaries, consists of both sub- and supraconscious elements—a personal unconscious, containing things forgotten or repressed, and a collective unconscious, containing all those psychic contents

peculiar not to one individual, but to many, and at the same time, i.e., either to a society, a people, or to mankind in general. Such contents are the "mystical collective ideas" . . . of the primitive . . . they include also the *generic concepts* of right, the State, religion, science, etc., current among civilized men . . . With civilized peoples, collective feelings are also bound up with certain collective ideas, such as for example the idea of God, justice, fatherland, etc.[4]

Psychic activity is expressed through four psychological functions: thought and feeling, sensation and intuition, the first pair rational, the second pair irrational, the functions of each pair being mutually exclusive. One of these four functions is usually dominant in the differentiated or "specialized" consciousness of civilized man. For example, if the dominant function is thinking, then feeling is submerged in the undifferentiated realm of the unconscious, while sensation and intuition become secondary and tertiary functions, participating in varying degrees in both conscious and unconscious activities. The individual psyche displays also a readiness of response that operates selectively and becomes a

4. *Psychological Types,* trans. H. G. Baynes (New York: Harcourt, Brace and Company, 1923), p. 530.

constellated *habitus,* or attitude, of which there are two types: extroversion, or a turning outward of libido upon objects; and introversion, or the turning inward of libido, the latter expressing a negative relation of subject to object. An attitude is acquired in connection with the dominant function and, combined with it, determines the psychological type—as, for example, the extroverted thinking type, the introverted intuitive type, and so on.

Ideally the four functions and the two attitudes should be harmonized during the various stages of life in accordance with the systole and diastole of the life process; but outer adaptation is nearly always preferred to inner adaptation. Since society today exalts extroversion, introversion often occurs according to the law of *enantiodromia,* by which an overly developed function passes into its opposite. Such introversion is likely to be an involuntary disaster rather than a voluntary turning inward for purposes of self-discovery. Jung considers voluntary introversion a natural and desirable stocktaking for the middle-aged adult, since youth and early maturity are normally periods of outer adaptation. He therefore regards involuntary introversion as an unconscious revolt against the restraints of the dominant function.

In people of highly differentiated consciousness, the dominant function often rules their lives, forming a hard shell which the ego wears like a mask and which serves as a kind of two-dimensional surface of the psyche. Jung calls this mask the *persona* and defines it as the role that the individual plays in society. From it a man derives his feeling of identity. It is really an excerpt from the general collectivity, however, and reflects the external world rather than real individuality. It largely shuts a person off from the shadow side of his nature as well as from his unrealized potentialities. Knowing himself but slenderly, the man who identifies himself with his persona is in danger of involuntary introversion and inner cleavage. Should this occur, a regressive movement of libido inevitably follows.

Regression and progression are contrary movements of libido with reference to the reciprocal activities of the conscious and unconscious layers of the psyche. Like physical energy, libido is di-polar and functions under the regulatory principle of "opposites," from which come the dynamic tensions of psychic life. Progression is the daily advance of the process of psychic adaptation to social norms. It is not an evolution but a movement forward as time flows backward. In contrast, regression is characterized by failure to reconcile the opposites and results in the turning back of libido into the unconscious. Jung says that "regression leads to the necessity of an adaptation to the soul, the inner world of the psyche." [5] This inner adaptation differs profoundly from the outer adaptation required by psychoanalysis, with its three stages of confession, explanation, and education. Inner adaptation involves transformation, or the formulation of a new weltanschauung.

Jung attributed the prevalence of neurosis today among people of highly differentiated consciousness to the psychic insufficiency of Western culture. He regarded the idea of deity as a psychological fact rather than a metaphysical truth (though he does not deny validity to religion) and said that by far the greatest number of his neurotic patients over thirty-five experienced inner cleavage because they uncon-

5. *Contributions to Analytical Psychology*, trans. H. G. and C. F. Baynes (New York: Harcourt, Brace and Company, 1928), p. 39.

sciously felt a need for a "highest value"—something in which to believe. For the most part, it is impossible to reanimate a dead faith in the overly conscious neurotic: "The modern man abhors dogmatic postulates taken on faith and the religions based upon them. He holds them valid only in so far as their knowledge-content seems to accord with his own experience of the deeps of psychic life. He wants to know—to experience for himself." [6] Jung therefore looks to psychology to re-establish the validity of psychic experience and to assist individuals who suffer from the general deterioration of values to discover within themselves the possibility of a religious experience.

The process by which such a discovery can be made is individuation. It is "the process of forming and specializing the individual nature; in particular, it is the development of the psychological individual as a differentiated being from the general collective psychology." [7] As the way to integration, it is bound up with what Jung calls the "transcendent function," a mode of reconciling opposites through the mediation of a class of symbols which are rooted in the collective unconscious and which appear in dreams—most frequently in those of neurotics. These symbols are primordial images or archetypes of the collective unconscious—automatic, inherited, and universal ways of thinking and feeling. Jung says that they have an "authentic religious function" and that through them a transformation may be brought about in the attitude of an individual which will lead to the development of a constructive outlook toward life.

Inaccessible to consciousness and independent of the will,

6. *Modern Man in Search of a Soul*, p. 239.
7. *Psychological Types*, p. 561.

these images are potentially capable of recapitulating (in dreams or other psychic phenomena) the history of the human psyche, somewhat in the way the human embryo recapitulates man's biological evolution. But there are important differences: the archetypes have no necessary sequence, and they function as autonomous complexes which may erupt into consciousness at any time. They represent symbolically the universal and timeless leitmotivs of the human psyche: they are the "big dreams" of humanity, "the buried treasure from which mankind has ever and always created, out of which have been drawn its gods and its demons, and all those most urgent and mighty thoughts without which man ceases to be man." [8] Symbolic of psychic conflict, irrational and archaic in form, they are mechanisms that have achieved autonomy owing to a blockage in the movement of libido into consciousness. The regressive movement thus takes the form of an encounter with demonic forces. Actually, however, the archetypes are "psychic organs," and their sole function is to give a man a vision of himself.

These primordial images are comparatively few in number, the chief being the *persona*, the *shadow*, the *anima* (man's feminine soul image), the *animus* (woman's masculine soul image), the *puer eternus*, the *mana* personality, and such theriomorphic forms as the snake (viper, serpent, dragon), the bull, and the dog. In addition to these human and animal figures, there are such natural phenomena as wood (the woods, a forest, a tree), the garden, the sun, the moon, the earth, and the ocean (or water in any form). Certain abstract and geometric figures like the circle, the

8. *Two Essays on Analytical Psychology*, trans. H. G. and C. F. Baynes (New York: Dodd, Mead and Company, 1928), p. 68.

sphere, the square, and the quaternity also appear in this phenomenology—these forms being the reconciling symbols of individuation, or hieroglyphs of a superordinate Self, mandalas.

In the dreams and visions of the neurotic, the archetypes by means of their "transcendent function" enact the drama of individuation and thus make available to consciousness quantities of libido. At the same time, the ego is displaced as the center of consciousness. This drama is analogous to ancient rites of initiation, such as the Eleusinian mysteries, each "image" representing an autonomous complex projected upon the screen of consciousness as an actor. For example, the persona symbolizes the conscious habitude with which the ego has been identified, while the shadow represents evil and antithetical personality traits. Encounter with the shadow opens up the unconscious.

A man's anima is a projection of his "soul"—the feminine and unconscious aspects of his nature. Jung regards the psyche as androgynous, and the anima therefore is contrasexual. She is really the feminine form of the shadow and becomes a kind of mistress-goddess, endowed with secret and magical powers. The ultimate purpose of the drama is to secure the anima's transformation into a function of relation between the conscious and unconscious parts of the psyche and thus to enable a man to know himself. The *puer eternus* is an androgynous "wonder child," representing the unrealized potentialities in the unconscious, and his appearance is therefore a symbol of rebirth. The *mana* personality "is the powerful man in the form of hero, chief, magician, medicine man, and saint, the lord of spirits, the friend of gods." As the psychopomp, he may become the "god image."

Jung recommends on psychological grounds that this figure not be transformed into a god image, because such transformation leads to new projections and inevitably divides again into god and devil. If the individual is to maintain his own "specific gravity," it will not be by "becoming the unresisting shuttlecock of unconscious forces." [9] Aspirations to godhead and leagues with Satan inflate the ego. A man needs to discover and realize his total self, to recognize that he is both finite and infinite—"a living something."

This something, though strange to us, is yet so near; it is altogether ourselves, and yet unrecognizable, a virtual middlepoint of such a mysterious constitution that it can demand anything, relationship with animals and with gods, with crystals and with stars, without causing us to wonder, without even exciting our disapproval. This something demands all that and more, and therefore, with nothing in our hands which could fairly be opposed to these claims, it is surely wiser to listen to this voice.

I have called this middle-point the self . . . It might just as well be called "the god in us." [10]

In the mandalas constructed by his patients, Jung noted two peculiarities, one of which he interpreted as modern man's actual inability to project the god image. Instead of the figure of a deity in the center of these reconciling symbols, "It is a star, a sun, a flower, a cross of equal branches, a precious stone, a bowl filled with water or wine, a serpent coiled up, or a human being but never a god." [11] The other distinguishing feature of the mandalas was the emphasis

9. *Ibid.*, p. 263.
10. *Ibid.*, p. 265.
11. *Psychology and Religion*, Terry Lectures, 1937 (New Haven: Yale University Press, 1938), p. 97.

upon quaternity, an emphasis pointing to an unconscious effort to replace the Christian symbol of the Trinity by one that will unite the female productive principle with the masculine principles of creativity, power, and light. In both of these details, modern mandalas are closer to the conceptions of medieval alchemical philosophy than to Christian dogma. It is no wonder, then, that Jung often refers to the magician Faust, or that he sees in Goethe's tragedy an alchemical drama of psychic transformation—an effort to bring together high and low and all the other pairs of opposites.

There seems to me no question but that *Doctor Faustus Lights the Lights* is a dream vision and a drama of individuation. Analysis of the dynamics of the opera reveals that the movement of the action is far away from traditional dramatic narrative, much closer to what can only be called psychic processes. It bears, however, less resemblance to the associational sequences of stream of consciousness than to the clear but illogical progressions and transformations of dreams, or perhaps the stasis of psychosomatic trauma. There is much, indeed, in the stage directions and action to suggest psychopathological conditions rarely encountered outside a mental hospital. For example, the intermittent play of the electric lights, represented by a ballet, calls for a choreography of intricately contrived and patterned rhythms suggestive of the mechanical movements of automata; the abrupt arrivals and departures of Mephisto, the girl called Marguerite Ida and Helena Annabel, and the man from over the seas mark what would seem to be the alternating subjective states of inertia and activity in schizophrenia. There is progression, too, like the prolonged pathological condition medically known as a fugue and characterized by wandering and other unusual actions of which, later, the individual has no recollection. In spite of these suggestions of psychotic disaster, however, the total action of the play results in a new condition of harmony and integration.

Briefly summarized, the three acts and six scenes of *Doctor Faustus* tell the following story. One should remember that it is an interior action, and that all the characters are functions or complexes within one human psyche.

A man variously called Faust, Faustus, and Doctor Faustus has invented electric lights, but finds that he is thoroughly bored with them. The whole transaction in which he supposedly sold his soul to the devil was a mere self-deception, committed in ignorance long ago. Now he believes neither in the reality of his soul nor in the existence of the devil. But he is exasperated by the continuous presence of Mephisto, then by the successive appearances of a dog, a boy, and a mysterious maiden named Marguerite Ida and Helena Annabel. The girl, who is bitten by a viper, comes to him to be cured. Though he cannot see her, he is persuaded to make the attempt and succeeds in restoring her to health by hypnotic methods.

Some time later, Marguerite Ida and Helena Annabel, having entered upon a life of devotion, sits in a niche in candlelight, wearing a halo, an artificial viper beside her. As the chorus tells the story of her bite and vicarious cure, and during the performance of a grand ballet of lights, a stranger from over the seas arrives and almost succeeds in wooing her away from the artificial viper. He is stopped, however, by Mephisto. In the meantime, Faust-Faustus-

Doctor Faustus has also been living in retirement. His three personalities are now completely separated, so that when rumor reaches him of the maiden's claim to be able to turn night into day—a power he had insisted was his alone—Doctor Faustus admits that he is not the only inventor and disappears into the crowd surrounding her as she sits enthroned beside the man from over the seas.

The quiet of the scene is disturbed by the arrival of Mephisto, who challenges the value of the maiden's light and creates an uproar, to which Faust, the boy, and the dog are invisible witnesses. Though nothing is apparently settled, Faustus enters into private negotiations with Mephisto to go to hell by himself. Mephisto assures him that he must commit a sin, whereupon he kills the boy and the dog with the aid of a real viper, and now declares that he is completely free from Mephisto: he can go to hell alone. But Mephisto suggests that Faustus become young again and take the girl with him. The transformation occurs, but Marguerite Ida and Helena Annabel rejects him and faints into the arms of the man from over the seas. In the final tableau the man from over the seas stands with her in his arms, while Mephisto carries Faustus down to hell. A little boy and girl, who first appeared in attendance upon Mephisto, sing a song in which they address the man from over the seas as Mr. Viper.

The following correlation of the characters with Jung's archetypes of the collective unconscious indicates in a general way the function of each "image" in the processes of introversion and individuation.

Faust—the protagonist of the play; the one in whose mind the action takes place; the totality of the Faustian psyche as well as the split personality. A name rather than a person, he is specifically referred to at the beginning of the play, and again in act III, scene ii, where he may actually speak—though the stage directions seem deliberately confused here. Probably he is a silent figure on the stage throughout the opera as the locus of the action—in which case he would be indistinguishable in appearance from the "selves" to whose behavior he is an audience. In this capacity he is both one and many. For the audience, he is the "wise old man," the psychopomp. At the moment, he has entered upon a stage of regressive introversion. He is one form of Faust's SUPERORDINATE SELF.

Faustus—the EGO of Faust; symbolic of the conscious will and the subjective aspects of personality. As the self-consciousness of Faust, he is on the stage a good deal of the time and is the central figure in the last struggle with Mephisto, who carries him down to hell at the end of the play. Drained of energy by the activities of libido, he sways between a desire to be lost in the crowd and a longing to assert his own point of view. Thus he wavers between hope and despair, and it is he who kills the boy and the dog and tries to take Marguerite Ida and Helena Annabel to hell with him. He is too changeable to have any character, except that of feeble opposition.

Doctor Faustus—the PERSONA of Faust; his social personality; the mask by which he knows himself and is known. As the face that Faust shows to the world, he represents thought itself, Faust's dominant function, which has been almost completely extroverted and consequently is confounded by the question, "What am I?"—a question Faust has involuntarily been compelled to raise with the eruption of Mephisto from the unconscious, in the guise of a traditional religious belief he had discarded in his extroverted activities as a scientist and inventor. He represents authority—the authority of reason and of order; consequently he is full of contradictions when he tries to unite instinct, evolutionary development, and an infallible, omniscient authority. Like the ego, from whom he is at first scarcely distinguishable, he is driven from one position to another and finally simply disappears in the crowd, reason not being a function of personality but of the human genus. He is mistaken for the god image, however, both by the public and by Marguerite Ida and Helena Annabel.

Mephisto—Faust's SHADOW; the dark half of his psyche, projected, and containing all of his undesirable traits; the complementary image of his persona-ego and the embodiment of feeling, the function of Faust's psyche that has been submerged in the unconscious. As the spirit that denies and the lord of counter-positions, he represents a "complex," completely independent of Faust's will, and his actions are aimed at embarrassing the persona. He reappears at intervals throughout the play and casts doubts upon the truth of the candlelight and the power of the viper. Though he loses everything else, he gets Faust's ego in the final moment. Equivocal, and multiordinal, Mephisto is ingratiating, oily-tongued, and deceitful. As a libido image, he unwittingly assists in the process of individuation in his function of "adversary." The master-bondsman relationship he tries to preserve toward both the ego and the persona suggests that he is to be associated with all that appears necessitated in experience.

Marguerite Ida and Helena Annabel—the ANIMA of Faust; a compound symbol of the eternal feminine in all its aspects. *Marguerite* is, of course, the girl destroyed by Faust's inordinate sensual passion—the "pearl" or treasure that became expendable in the course of his quest for knowledge. *Ida,* whose name suggests the Freudian concept of the id, is the will-to-power in general terms. Mount Ida, the seat of the worship of Cybele, is a place, not a person, the scene of orgiastic celebrations of the Great Mother of the Gods, whom classical antiquity knew as Rhea, wife of Cronos, and daughter of Uranos and Gaea. *Helena* is the mythological Helen of Greek story who bears Euphorion to Faust in

Part Two of Goethe's tragedy. She represents the transformation of libido into an ideal order. As the classic type of man's aspirations toward the perfection of nature, she expresses creative energy fulfilling itself in the imitation of nature. *Annabel,* the "fair Anna," suggests by derivation the name Hannah, which in Hebrew means "grace." She is the Anna Perenna of Italian tradition and also the mother of the Virgin Mary. In fact, throughout the ancient world "Anna" was the commonest name for the Great Mother of the Gods. According to Roman tradition, Anna Perenna was a sister of Belus, or Bel. As a place name, Bel bears somewhat the same significance that Ida does, in that it refers to a location originally associated with religious worship of an earth-god. The initials MIHA suggest *maya,* the Hindu word for the manifestation of the female energy of the deity, the power behind the veil of appearances, personified under many different names. In Greek, Maia was the daughter of Atlas and the mother of Hermes. As a common noun, it meant mother, nurse, and midwife. A metaphor for the totality of the psyche, the anima represents the four psychic functions: Marguerite, feeling; Ida, sensation; Helena, thought; Annabel, intuition. Her dichotomy recalls the little world (personal history) and the great world (universal and collective experience). In the course of the play the anima is born, sins, is saved, is deified, and is finally transformed into the world of Ideas.

The Man from Over the Seas—a redeemer figure and therefore Faust's SUPERORDINATE SELF in its essence; the antithesis of the ego, the persona, and the shadow; the actualizing of the *puer eternus.* United with the anima at the end of the opera, he symbolizes the movement forward out of the unconscious of Faust's inferior function, feeling, and the reconciliation of the contending elements in his psyche. He is the positive pole in experience— the affirmation of life. Contaminated by the shadow at first, so that he appears excessively sentimental, confused with the per-

sona so that he seems to have supernatural power, he is identified with the sun (natural energy) and with the viper (experience). As the transformed libido of the individuated Faust, he
is "immediacy itself." In the struggle for possession of the anima
he displaces, simply by his presence, both the ego and the persona. Called Viper-Sun, he is both destroyer and preserver.

A *Dog*—a theriomorphic form of the PUER ETERNUS whose
epiphany it precedes and ushers in. It represents libido in its
conservative form, but also symbolizes the binding force of instinct and the compulsive drive of animal appetite. Gertrude
Stein's favorite analogue for human nature, the dog manifests
none of its primordial ferocity. Conscious, but incapable of self-
consciousness, it is just itself throughout the play, following its
instincts and obeying its master. It barks or wags its tail with
excitement, and says "thank you" again and again to show its
dependence on the external world. Being unable to distinguish
between electric light and daylight, it can only say, "My my what
a sky," when the stage is flooded with the electric lights. It is no
longer able to see the moon, owing to the artificial illuminations
that flicker all the time. The dog, therefore, represents animal
nature domesticated and habit-bound. Stein said that human
nature was not natural, thus calling attention to the changes in
habit brought by cultural development.

A *Boy*—the PUER ETERNUS; a hermaphroditic libido symbol, in-
dicating Faust's unrealized potentialities; a form of the child-
hero, or infant god, whose life is fraught with danger. Always a
hopeful image, according to Jung, the *puer eternus* is a positive
symbol and anticipates the superordinate self. Along with the
dog, he is sacrificed, in this version of the Faust story, by the ego.
He has analogues in the infant Zeus, the infant Dionysus, the
infant Hermes, the boy Cupid, and the Christ Child. Jung points
out that one of the stages of individuation is often marked by
regression to the land of childhood, a symbol of the desire for

rebirth. In Goethe's *Faust*, Part Two, the boy figure has three different forms: the young charioteer in the allegorical masquerade of act I, the elfish and elusive Homunculus of act II, and the child Euphorion (son of Helena and Faust) of act III.

A Country Woman with a Sickle—Hecate, with the crescent moon; a symbol of fertility and growth but also of emasculation and death; an equivocal figure to be linked with undifferentiated libido and with superstition and darkness. She is earthy, practical, and full of folk wisdom, and it is she who sends the anima to the persona to be cured.

A Boy and a Girl—symbols of the polarity of all things in the universe that come into being and pass away; the opposites that, out of conflict, tension, and resolution, preserve the continuity of both natural and psychic life. Unlike the *puer eternus*, who represents pure potentiality, the boy and the girl belong to the realm of process. They first appear behind Mephisto, but they always address the man from over the seas, whom they call Mr. Viper, begging him to remember that one is a boy, the other a girl, and urging him to "Listen to me," thus expressing the decisions we make at every moment of our lives. They naively express difference, equality, and harmony and by their repetitions point to the broad recurrences in our experience.

A Viper—a theriomorphic symbol of libido; an ambivalent symbol of experience, pointing equally toward life and death. Its bite is the wound that activates fear and hope. The serpent in the garden and the snake in neurotic dreams, it is also a surrogate for the sun, a fertility symbol, and an image of the Self. Creative and destructive, it is associated with the redeemer image, the man from over the seas, who is called "Viper-Sun." As a transformation image, the viper is associated with the art of healing (the serpents on the caduceus) and with renewal.

An Artificial Viper—a man-made image of the real viper; a work of art. It symbolizes the forms of repentance, contrition, and confession in the Catholic Church, as well as the ritual and liturgy by which the terrors of religious doubt, guilt, and fear of death are overcome—particularly formal prayer and conformity to dogma and external authority. Very "pretty" and harmless, the artificial viper also represents traditional acceptance of an unexamined and unexperienced belief. Incapable of inflicting injury, it tends to make people forget the real viper, but it has great power and at one point becomes the anima's "might," only to disappear after the advent of the man from over the seas.

A Chorus—the voice of society and its opinions; all that has been learned rather than felt. As opposed to the vital inner life of the psyche, the chorus repeats what it has been told or what it has heard. When it is on the stage, it forms an audience for the action as well as an echo for the voice of habit and external authority. Its views change with those of the Faustian "personalities," approving or disapproving according to the dominant attitude.

The Ballet of Electric Lights—a complicated symbol with many levels of meaning: the movement of libido inward and outward, forward and back; the activity of conceptual thought and directed thinking; the rational and scientific intellect in general. It is opposed to candlelight (the light of traditional religion), to moonlight (the halflight of superstition and folk wisdom, the cause of madness), and to darkness (the abyss of the unconscious). The ballet of lights is first associated with Faust's persona, but the lights grow bright, flicker, glow, or go out according to whether the action is taking place in Faust's conscious or unconscious mind. Their artificiality is contrasted to the sun, which symbolizes both the light of nature and the light of intuition. They disappear before the last scene, which takes place under a noonday sun.

Classification of the Jungian archetypes is comparatively

easy but interpretation is another matter, for, as Jung says, these images can mean anything and must be referred to the character and circumstances of the individual in whose dreams they appear. The scenario of *Doctor Faustus* lays great stress upon the motions and relative positions of the actors on the stage—whether they appear at the left or right, behind or in front, facing one another or turned away. These directions seem to refer to the movement of libido and serve to keep the audience informed as to the object of Faust's attention and the relation between his conscious and unconscious activities. Thus motion toward the left indicates regression; toward the right, progression. Similarly, contrasts between extroversion and introversion are represented by actual location on the stage, the projections appearing in the foreground, the withdrawals at the rear. The ballet of electric lights communicates the moods that accompany the movements and transformations of libido. Thus we learn a good deal about Faust from visualizing these movements and relationships.

In the long and expository first scene, the consciousness of Faust is represented by a room with a door and windows; his dream world occupies the stage before it. He stands in the doorway gazing outward, a blaze of electric lights behind him, so that we know he is really at the threshold of his unconscious, looking backward into himself and away from the civilization created by the Enlightenment. Either beside him or standing in the windows, his persona (Doctor Faustus) and his ego (Faustus) are also confronting this inner world, which is projected in the form of Mephisto, his shadow, whose appearance marks the onset of neurosis or perhaps even the threat of schizophrenia.

We learn of the cause of Faust's introversion from the persona. He has been losing sleep; suddenly confronted by the apparition of the devil, he is filled with a sense of guilt and fear, though he knows that the spectre is nothing but a creation of his own mind. He sees no use anyway in the electric lights, since they give no new insights into the meaning of life. Instead, they have taken away all his beliefs, except his overvaluation of his own rational consciousness. His hubris comes out when he answers the question, "What am I?" by affirming dogmatically, "I am Doctor Faustus who knows everything and can do everything," thus showing that he has made a god of his persona. He has the scientist's contempt for subjective phenomena, explaining that once he believed in gods and demons—but that was because, in his hurry to master nature's secrets, he had filled the gap between the facts and his knowledge by "spirits," and had imagined that he "saw" and "needed" the devil. Since then, he has discovered scientific method and has proved that the cosmos is a mechanism. There is no "snake to grind under one's heel," no death, no life, no breath, no hope. His ego is equally nihilistic but as deflated as the persona is inflated, for the presence of the shadow has brought home to him the truth that "light however bright will never be other than light"—that in spite of his gift for planning and organizing, he has achieved no real mastery over destiny. Both the ego and the persona agree that the supposed sale of Faust's soul is highly problematical, for they do not believe in the soul, nor do they see how, if it was sold, Faust could still have one.

During this first encounter, Mephisto, the shadow, is very familiar, addressing the persona as "Dear Doctor Faustus" and trying to pat his arm. Since Doctor Faustus, as a materialistic scientist, is an extroverted thinking type, his shadow personality is motivated by his undeveloped function of feeling. Thus Mephisto seems to be a sentimental quibbler, yet fascinating and powerful. His function in the process of introversion and individuation is to bring about the collapse of the persona, whom he flatters and tempts to intellectual arrogance, at the same time threatening to "while away whatever there is to give away." The impact of his presence is sufficient to make the ego feel that he is only a kind of shadow himself moving among shadows. In the violence of frustration, he kicks at the shadow, thus intensifying regression and evoking other and more primitive archetypes from the collective unconscious.

Amid an ensuing grand ballet of electric lights, symbolic of man's biological and social evolution, Faust's dog appears as representative both of instinct and of acquired habits. Primarily social, the dog assumes a propitiatory, dependent attitude toward the world, its "thank you" being a gesture of self-protection as well as of acceptance. To symbolize its animal warmth, the electric lights "glow," while Doctor Faustus sings a duet with the dog in celebration of the electric lights and petitions to be "bathed" in them—a prayer that suggests Faust's yearning to be merged with the "All." His eyes are dazzled by the brilliance of the lights and "nothing" comes, an ambiguous reference to the primal, undifferentiated libido or to the collective unconscious. The ego, less concerned with origins than with destiny, meditates upon the freedom of the will and thus summons out of the unconscious the *puer eternus*, a little boy, who comes in and immediately begins to play with the dog. An image of the childhood of Faust, the boy also represents the infancy of mankind, the possibility of spiritual rebirth, and the freedom of the human mind.

The passage that follows seems to involve the gradual development of any primitive society. In such societies the "medicine man," by separating himself from the group, establishes and regulates its conduct in relation to the sun, the moon, and the cycle of the seasons. The Faust persona, who seems to represent such a *mana* personality, first sings a song asking the boy and dog to leave him alone and then resolves not to think. The ego, given over to intuition, ignores the warning that "when the hay has to be cut every day then there is the devil to pay," and listens to his own thoughts. Suddenly he cries that he hears "her" calling. "She" is to sing about all kinds of light, and her name is Marguerite Ida and Helena Annabel. Thus the differentiated consciousness conceives of the divine soul and threatens the authority of the persona, the established law and reason. In spite of Doctor Faustus' denial of "her" name and power, the dog, the boy, Faustus, and the chorus declare that they believe in her.

If we regard Doctor Faustus, the persona, as a medicine man or an elite personality, this scene seems to condense tremendous periods of human history, portraying the general process by which an individual intuition arises from the collective unconscious and returns to it after it is formulated. Not primarily important, since the play is essentially a psychic monodrama, the historical dimension in *Doctor Faustus Lights the Lights* is analogous to the allegorical suggestions of the wanderings, fate, and aspirations of whole peoples that one finds in many legendary figures—Abraham, for example, in Genesis or, closer to home, the Faust of

European legend. (A similar multiplicity of reference, including the historical, is found in Kafka's work: in less than ten pages "The Hunger Artist" condenses not only the psychic plight of one individual, but at least a thousand years of European history—artistic and religious.) I do not wish to overemphasize this element of historical allegory in Stein's little play. To some readers it may seem irrelevant, and those who perceive it will enjoy working out its implications for themselves. But in the following discussion I have included a tentative allusion, here and there, to the level of historical meaning I have sensed in the work.

The second scene dramatizes the birth of Faust's "soul image," his anima. It is difficult not to think of her as a real girl—immature, full of feminine wiles, but unconscious of her power. Furthermore, since Faust identifies his ego with his persona, she is probably also meant to be the real woman onto whom Faust projects his own unconscious feminine qualities. We can regard this scene, I think, as a realization of the "dream girl." Since she is an autonomous complex, she is undeveloped, naive, highly emotional, and deficient in judgment. She has a practical side, however, which suggests that she is actually playing a part. She appears in a dark wood, lush with undergrowth and with wild beasts lurking everywhere. At first she is fearful, longing for authority and security ("a chair with a carpet under it"). Then she shrieks hysterically, "I am here I am not there and I am Marguerite Ida and Helena Annabel and it is not well." Wandering about in the darkness, she calls and calls, and finally perceives a light in the distance, toward which she is moving when she is bitten by a viper.

The viper bite probably symbolizes here the immature and deficient eroticism that may be observed, according to

Jung, in any middle-aged man who identifies his ego with his persona and who is consequently a prey to irrational impulses in his private life. In general the snake or viper, like the arrow, symbolizes introversion—that inward turning of attention and libido which sometimes brings death by poison but, now and then, healing and salvation. In this context, however, the viper bite has the immediate significance of a traumatic—and sexual—temptation. (An involuntary crisis of introversion is, if not caused by sexual indiscretion and attendant feelings of guilt, at least quite often accompanied by the onset of irresistible feelings of this sort.) It should not be forgotten that Marguerite Ida and Helena Annabel is the anima, the still unpurged soul image of the total Faust personality. Since the dark wood is one of the primordial symbols of the unconscious, and the anima the psychic organ for inward awakening, the episode symbolizes the complete emergence and activation of the protagonist's inner life.

The anima is more curious than frightened by the viper bite. She is just debating whether she has been stung or bitten when she encounters a country woman with a sickle— the archetypal image of fructification and death but in this context probably a symbol of public opinion, which is apt to recommend conformity to the moral discipline of the church. The old woman sends the anima to Doctor Faustus because he has the reputation of being able to "kill the poison." Still trying to decide whether vipers sting or bite, the girl trips off, rather hoping that Doctor Faustus will "make it a bite."

The third scene takes place in Doctor Faustus' room, in an atmosphere that savors equally of the confessional and the turn-of-the-century nerve specialist's darkened consultation room. In the company of the dog and the boy, who are asleep and dreaming, the persona is lost in speculations concerning the nature of identity and moral responsibility. As he murmurs in despair, "What am I oh what am I?" the anima calls to him, and soon enters, as the electric lights glow softly. Doctor Faustus is strangely unable to see her. Her appeal to him to cure her is like that of the lamia, who always secures mastery over her lover by appealing to either his strength or his pity. Mischievously, she questions whether he is the godlike person he thinks himself and then demands that he cure her, shrieking that he has sold his soul but she still has hers and may die and go to hell.

Since Doctor Faustus is the "medicine man," he may be a practitioner of either the cure of bodies or the cure of souls. The following passage may be read, for example, as a description of the way in which one wins forgiveness for sin through the mediation of the disciplines of the church, and the "cure" in this case is the grace conferred upon the penitent. But Doctor Faustus is the persona and may even be an early psychiatrist, who has no connected insights into psychic processes. He claims that he has sold his soul "here there and everywhere" for "thought," and so he can only deal with visible objects. Stubbornly maintaining that he "gave the light" and that it is both "right" and "bright," he begs to be left alone to his physical researches. When he is asked what use there is in his having been to hell—that is, in his scientific labors—if he cannot cure the anima, he pleads that he cannot see her. She begs him not to see her but to cure her, thus enticing him to further pretensions, and he ultimately undertakes to heal her, employing the artifice of hypnotic suggestion. This takes the form of an incantatory rhyme, "Enough said, / You are not dead," echoed by the chorus and finally whispered by the anima, who has almost swooned away amid the flicker of the lights.

In this scene it is possible to see modern man wavering between a completely naturalistic view of psychic processes and a completely supernatural view of the soul, a conflict that has brought the priest and the psychotherapist into close, if uncomfortable, proximity. It is no surprise, then, that the second act presents the status of religion in the modern world. As in the first act, there is a suggestion of an historical orientation.

At first there is no particular location designated, though the place might well be a village square surrounding a cathedral or public shrine at the end of the middle ages. The crowd speaks rather disrespectfully of "Nell" (Annabel?), who has accepted a "salted almond" but is a "fatty" and does not pay for it. There are also casual references to butter, the butcher, and "silver sell," which suggest (especially the pun on "sell") the *quid pro quo* involved in the consecration of the priest and the practical value attributed to the Mass. Then we are told that now "they" can "spell," perhaps a reminder of the importance of printing in the Protestant Reformation. The women find it "extraordinary" and a "relief" that Marguerite Ida and Helena Annabel has four names. Apparently they had thought her name was Marguerite Ida only. "Of course her names is Marguerite Ida and Helena Annabel," someone says, revealing the layman's confused efforts to grasp the sacred mysteries. References to Doctor Faustus, whose miraculous cure is said to have healed the anima of the viper bite, attribute to him the power of priestly authority. The systematizing, conceptualizing intellect has here been metamorphosed into the Pope image and stands for ecclesiastical infallibility and apostolic succession. Like

children reciting the catechism, the crowd repeats the story
of the anima's encounter with the viper and her vicarious
cure.

Now a curtain is pulled open at one corner of the stage to
reveal Marguerite Ida and Helena Annabel, wearing a halo
and encircled by candlelight, an artificial viper beside her.
As she sits and "waits," the chorus sings a song filled with
questions and contradictory opinions, reminiscent of the
Protestant Reformation and the sectarian controversies it
engendered:

> There she is
> And what is there
> The viper that bit her
> No silly no
> How could he be there
> This is not a viper
> This is what is like a viper . . .

The theriomorphic symbol of sin and death, fertility and
rebirth, the viper in an artificial form embodies these ideas
in a work of art—namely, the creed, ceremonials, and euchar-
istic rites of the Catholic Church, the function of which is
to objectify and control the creative and lawless dark forces
of libido. Possibly the artificial viper also stands for the
rational attitude that denies the mystery of transubstantia-
tion and regards the Mass as commemorative rather than
efficacious. For the rationalist, the conflict between good and
evil remains unresolved; for the believer, the drama of sacrifice and redemption is projected outward upon a redeemer
and backward in time to the life of the historical Christ,
while salvation becomes a divine gift to be bestowed here-
after. As one of Faust's dreams, this scene reveals his irrational yearning for faith, while it also implies that he would

like to escape from direct religious experience by taking refuge in a creed unacceptable to his conscious mind. The attitude of devotion has a good effect, however; it activates a new archetype—the hitherto latent function of feeling, projected in the man from over the seas, a stranger, arriving at dawn after a night journey by water (the unconscious). This wanderer identifies himself with the sun and at once seeks to woo the anima away from the artificial viper.

He speaks in words that suggest in their sentimentality the Rousseauistic child of nature and the pantheism that inspired the nature worship and excesses of feeling of the romantic movement. His antipathy to the anima's preoccupation with the artificial viper expresses a positive attitude toward experience: "What is a viper, a viper is a serpent and anybody has been bitten and not everybody dies and cries, and so why why say it all the time, I have been bitten I I I have been bitten by her bitten by her there she sits with her back to the sun and I have won I have won her I have won her." He urges her to "throw away the viper throw away the sun throw away the lights until there are none." Asking whether he is Doctor Faustus, she seems about to yield, for she drops the viper. But she immediately picks it up when Mephisto appears behind the man from over the seas, accompanied by a boy and a girl. The arrival of this trio seems to deny that the man from over the seas is "the only one" as he had claimed. The boy and the girl, apparently the "opposites" in familiar form, suggest that without contraries there is no progression.

As a stage in the process of individuation, this scene marks the restoration to Faust of the power of his own judgment. Here, for the first time, his superordinate Self begins to be differentiated from the various autonomous complexes or, rather, Faust seems to be on the verge of withdrawing them. In himself, however, the man from over the seas must not yet be regarded as this superordinate Self: he is the necessary charge of latent feeling—hitherto unconscious and undeveloped—which is required (in unison with other components of the psyche) to bring this Self to birth. The action at this point is very lively indeed (and very funny). While the boy and girl, with the assistance of the chorus, sing a song about "he is a boy I am a girl," addressed to "Mr. Viper," Mephisto dashes about the stage declaring that he has a will of iron ("I do what I do what I do, I do I do")—threatening everyone and challenging the anima's candlelight. She declares that "lights are all right but the viper is my might." During this part, as the ballet of lights rushes in and out, the man from over the seas stands aloof and smiling, saying only, "It is lovely to be at ease."

The last act contains two scenes, both of them set in Doctor Faustus' house, not his room, a difference implying that Faust's consciousness now has access to his unconscious mind. The first of these scenes portrays the final collapse of the persona; the second, the transformation of the anima into the function that relates the layers of Faust's psyche. The curtain rises upon the ego (Faustus), seated in Faust's chair in darkness, the dog and the boy beside him, the electric lights at the right to indicate that the movement of libido is upward from the unconscious. Drained of energy, the persona is dormant, but the ego is restless. He wants something—he does not know what, except that it is not "light," or "bright," or "sight," or "night," or "alright," and it has nothing to do with "me" or "she." He has no fear, but he is excessively bored with solipsism and freedom from care. It is as if he had passed through the stages of confession, explanation, and education, but has not yet achieved the stage of transformation which would give him a new world view. He still cannot find a highest value, though he would rather like to make "white" electric light. "Ah I do not like that word me," he murmurs. Then, in the vacuity of his own emptiness, he falls asleep as the dog and boy explain that all the mystery has departed from the world since the moon has lost her magical power.

Doctor Faustus, the sleeping persona, is aroused to defend his reputation only when a woman at the window shrieks that the anima now claims to be able to turn night into day. When he finally grasps that he is not the only one who can bring light out of darkness, he seems to welcome the news and goes out exclaiming, "Come on everyone, never again will I be alone come on come on everyone." His departure portrays Faust's recognition of the generic quality of the reasoning processes and is an admission that understanding depends upon feeling. With his disappearance, the ego (Faustus) is left alone with the dog and the boy—instinct and intuition.

The final scene occurs in brilliant sunlight. The anima is discovered seated beside the man from over the seas, their backs to the sun, in a noonday hush. We are therefore at the threshold of consciousness in the intermediate zone from which our ideas come. The encircling crowds are somnambulistic, some of them identifying the man from over the seas with Doctor Faustus, others contradicting this. Reality and vital experience seem very remote as others murmur confusedly, "Come come viper sun, we know no other one." In this passage, pantheism, sentimental naturalism, and religious dogma are jumbled together in an automatic and mechanical way, as if all distinctions had been lost. The people cannot remember any one but the man from over the seas; yet they have not forgotten the "sweet quiet viper" or Doctor Faustus, the boy, and the dog that said "thank you." They remember and forget, but they do not actually experience anything except a general feeling of affirmation: their perceptions have neither clarity nor intensity of feeling. In Jungian terms, the scene pictures the "circumambulation" that precedes the final stage of individuation and the construction of the mandala.

The condensation in the last part of the play makes summary very difficult. First the man from over the seas grows more lively and persuades the anima to forget that she has only four names in one. She confesses that she cannot "say" what is night and day, that she cannot "come" for anyone, but that "Who hears me knows me I am here." At this, the man from over the seas addresses her as "Dear me," whereupon Faust himself appears out of the gloom, accompanied by the boy and the dog. Unseen by the others, he becomes a witness of the ensuing action. His presence tells us that he recognizes the anima as his own unconscious and the man from over the seas as the herald of his superordinate Self. He is thus about to withdraw his projected illusions. Simultaneously, however, Mephisto usurps the center of the stage and begins to accuse everyone of deceiving him. His reappearance can best be understood in Jung's terms:

If you imagine someone who is brave enough to withdraw these projections, all and sundry, then you get an individual conscious of a pretty thick shadow. Such a man has saddled himself with new problems and conflicts. He has become a serious problem to himself, as he is now unable to say that *they* do this or that, *they* are wrong and *they* must be fought against. He lives in the "house of self-collection." Such a man knows that whatever is wrong in the world is in himself, and if he only learns to deal with his own shadow then he has done something real for the world . . . How can anyone see straight when he does not even see himself and that darkness which he himself carries unconsciously into all his dealings? [12]

With eveything divine or demonic now inside him, Faust is in great danger of ego inflation. There is a brief moment when he stands firmly against his shadow and speaks as Faust. Then the ego complains that "it is not ready yet" and wants to forget and "to be me myself all now." He talks as if the anima were no part of him. Assured by the shadow that she too will go to hell (apparently a gibe at Freudian and Calvinistic dogmas about the "evil unconscious" and original sin), Faustus expresses the wish to go to hell alone. But since he has sold his soul for a light, he does not know how. The shadow tells him to commit a sin—to kill something. Reluctantly, he kills the dog and the boy with the aid of the real viper, thus extinguishing sensation and intuition—an act representing the false asceticism that hopes to achieve power by the mortification of impulsive life. But the sacrificial act only strengthens his intellectual pride, so that when Mephisto says, "Have I nothing to do with you," he answers no and thus invites further temptation. The shadow immediately offers to rejuvenate him so that he can win the anima and take her to hell with him. But the anima is not to be deceived by the transformation that ensues. If he is young, then he is not Doctor Faustus, the identity of Faust—his personal history. And now she reveals herself in her true nature: "I am Marguerite Ida and Helena Annabel and I know no man or devil no viper and no light I can be anything and everything and it is always always alright."

12. *Psychology and Religion*, pp. 101-102.

As the key to those universal ideas that live in the collective unconscious, she is simply the creative principle itself—and therefore, in a sense, Faust's own "genius"—in its myriad transformations; she is not an image, but the possibility of images.

In the final tableau, the anima falls back fainting into the arms of the man from over the seas, while Mephisto carries Faustus down to hell. Thus in ceasing to be an autonomous complex, the anima loses her compulsive power to fascinate. But this apparent renunciation frees her to exercise her true function—that is, to serve as a virtual point between the conscious and unconscious levels of the human mind. She is wedded to the man from over the seas (who represents the access of libido that has emerged from the unconscious); taken together, this pair seems to represent the real Self. Such a consummation is impossible, however, unless the ego surrenders its position as the center of the psyche—a surrender symbolized here by Faustus's descent into hell. Hell (from Indo-European root KAL, to cover or conceal) here represents the depths of unconsciousness, the "hidden or unseen place." Now the boy and girl start the cycle over again. For in every human psyche the dynamics of the individuation process rest upon the natural polarities of sexual energy, which need to be transformed through introversion and contact with a new fund of libido from the unconscious. The last words in the opera belong to these children: "Please Mr. Viper listen to me he is he and she is she and we are we please Mr. Viper listen to me."

A few additional points may be suggested concerning the wedded pair that constitutes the real Self. Though it may seem difficult to think of the man from over the seas as an avatar, he is reminiscent of the Hindu deity Siva, the cosmic dancer and the god of the arts. It is worth noting that the root of the word "civilization" is the Sanskrit *siva,* meaning friendly or dear, and that the man from over the seas constantly uses this word "dear" of Marguerite Ida and Helena Annabel, whom he finally calls "Dear me." This usage does not describe the emotions of sexual love or the longing for what is not, but the treasuring and acceptance, for its own sake, of something that *is*—an aesthetic judgment that affirms or creates value. As the viper-sun, the man from over the seas represents the transformation of libido into feeling intensities. Marguerite Ida and Helena Annabel may be compared to Shakti, Siva's consort—the female principle of energy in Hinduism. The goddess whose myriad forms are known as "the divine Mothers," she symbolizes the active productive principle, in the sense that she is a contrasexual opposite necessary for the release of creative energy. Thus Marguerite Ida and Helena Annabel is analogous, perhaps, to the Platonic realm of creative ideas; but she seems even closer to Boehme's Sophia, the "eye of God," a far more dynamic concept. It would be possible to push the analogy between these Hindu deities and Gertrude Stein's hero and heroine further, but she did not intend to deify them. Rather she sought to present them as pyschic functions, symbolic of the invisible realities of the inner life.

As I understand *Doctor Faustus Lights the Lights,* the play contains no dogmatic postulates concerning theology, but affirms a "highest value" and identifies it with what the developed personality treasures. We need not be deceived by the coy banality of the "pretty pretty dear" phrases with which the man from over the seas addresses Marguerite Ida and Helena Annabel. In this *Faustus* of hers Gertrude Stein

is addressing our intelligence and intuition, not our conditioned, conventional feelings; and she makes this appeal,
in part, by a tone deliberately light and almost satirical, with
touches of farcical humor. In context, it is plain that she is
speaking of the "pearl without price," the "treasure hid in
a field," the one thing needful for which a man might well
lose the whole world—that is, in Biblical terms, the soul. In
more modern language one can speak of that contact with
the riches of racial wisdom and intuitive vision which possession of the key, the anima, confers upon the individual
Self. This is, of course, a deeply religious idea.

In *The Geographical History of America* Stein had distinguished between the empirical self (identity) and the individual consciousness that thinks, feels, and wills and acts
creatively. Identity is phenomenal appearance, external to
the reality of the Self, which has enclosed and shaped experience throughout the course of life. The Self is the
unfolding process of its own realization: "You are of course
never yourself" (EA, 68). This self-realizing potential has
nothing to do with age, history, or identity. In the course
of her meditations, she distilled out of experience a residue,
the "human mind," which she viewed as an impersonal,
transforming energy, somewhat like a catalytic agent, differentiated from the will-to-live and from causality. It approxi-
mates the Hindu conception of Bhakti, religious devotion,
but is an intensity of attention rather than worship of a deity.
Symbolically, in *Doctor Faustus*, Stein seems to represent
this human mind in the figure of Marguerite Ida and Helena
Annabel, who becomes individuated, so to speak, only when
joined to the emergent feeling function—the man from over
the seas. It would seem that Gertrude Stein dispensed with
the idea of a personal immortal soul, while preserving the

principle of individuation, and that similarly she dispensed
with the idea of a god endowed with personality, who can
be petitioned and propitiated.

In *Four in America,* she had emphasized the absence of
all formal aspects from what she called American religion.
For example, "American religion has no sky and why" (FIA,
30)—that is, the American does not believe in a future life
and has no system of theology to explain the cosmos. One
of her definitions makes God the incomparable: "American
religion is what they cannot compare with themselves" (FIA,
71). Here the meaning seems to be that Americans acknowledge a force free from time and causality, but do not endow
it with personality or objectify it in a creed. To be sure,
several million traditionally oriented church members in
this country might find these observations incomprehensible
as well as untrue. Yet genuine religion, for the masses of
men, is not what people think they believe about the cosmos
but, instead, those unconscious collective assumptions and
modes of feeling that are never questioned because they are
never noticed.

In spite of the dangers of oversimplification, therefore,
Gertrude Stein was probably right in believing that Oriental
and Occidental religious feelings and attitudes are united
in the genuine religion of America—at least if this is defined
in terms of those unconscious assumptions upon which people act. In the East, where the divine is usually conceived as
basically an Impersonal Absolute, human consciousness
tends to be anonymous and communal. Personality, in other
words, is not considered the highest category of reality, and
human personality is not emphasized and cherished. For
the masses, of course, this means only superstition, apathy,
and indifference to individualist values. At its highest level,

in the true sage or saint, such anonymity becomes the Nothing, or personal nonbeing, through a process of extreme introversion that treats personal consciousness as an illusion and emphasizes inaction and abnegation of the will. In the West, on the other hand, genuine introversion is exceedingly rare, and "introverted" is a term that implies, in popular belief, a certain neurotic incapacity for healthy living. The individual's thought, attention, and desire, in short, are normally focused on the external world of nature, society, objects, and the behavior of other men. Imperceptibly, however, science has ordered and systematized life until the individual is less a self than a statistic (John Doe or the man in the street). Thus the wheel has come full circle: the West also looks upon personal consciousness as an illusion—particularly in America, where mechanization and organization have largely concealed the activity of the individual as individual.

As a consequence, in spite of a political and religious tradition that sets a very high value on the category of personality and the worth of the individual, the mass American of the twentieth century is psychically undeveloped and lacking in true individuality. Thoroughly unconscious of his bondage to the collective unconscious, he prides himself on his freedom—a relative freedom from want and care which has released a good deal of psychic energy that might well be used in an effort toward growth and self-transcendence. But this energy is ordinarily used in random activities—play or crime or, at best, invention. America before the Second World War was consequently in the condition of "participation mystique": that is, the American unconscious was "archaic," primitive, lacking in self-awareness, and therefore habitually projected upon figures capable of carrying the load of the archetypes in their crudest form. Just as the unconscious of the medieval mass man was projected upon saints and devils, witches and the Virgin, so the American unconscious has been projected upon Hollywood movie stars, personalities in the news, and athletes. Individual feeling is almost extinct, and true individuation extremely rare. And so America has drawn closer to the East: the actuality is that the individual is sinking, even here, into the undifferentiated collective.

Latent in this unpleasant actuality, however, there is a new possibility. Several American sages, in the past century and a quarter, have seen that East and West might draw together in another fashion. Though in different ways, both Emerson and Whitman opposed to dogmatic religions a religious view that is Oriental in its conception of an objective creative principle manifesting itself as the individuating force in the human psyche. Like them, Gertrude Stein believed that Eastern objectivity and impersonality could be combined with Western subjectivity and individualism to constitute a religion in which the god image has been replaced by a kind of superordinate Self participating in an unlimited community. Rightly or wrongly, she thought America had begun to realize this religion, or at least had prepared the conditions for it. And she welcomed it as an expression of an ancient world view. She thought that Europeans had already felt its impact:

It is all over everywhere American religion is, not over or all over, but really everywhere. Now. Not over there, but there and everywhere, American religion is . . . American religion has spread. Yes it has. In Europe they think that nothing is there because the sky is there but in America they know it is there because there is no sky there . . . The European knows about the American sky not being a sky like that. O yes they do. They may say no but oh yes they do. (FIA, 72-73)

It seems to me that the man from over the seas in *Doctor Faustus Lights the Lights* embodies this possible American religion. As the present stage in the individuation of Western man, the man from over the seas receives into his arms the composite world process itself, the maya of appearances and the ground of actualization. Thus the European cultural tradition, symbolized by Doctor Faustus, becomes transfigured into its American avatar, who has cast off traditions and faces the future with "nothing" in his hands.

But *Doctor Faustus Lights the Lights* is a fantasy, not a work of history. Gertrude Stein did not believe that this transformation would usher in some utopia. Her point is that man's potentialities now lie in a reawakening of the inner life rather than in institutions, since human nature is externally bound by the dialectical processes that move endlessly between the poles of individualism and communism. The great problem is for man to face his shadow, his own desert places; to recognize that "the real ideas are not the relation of human beings as groups but a human being to himself inside him" (EA, 206). No amount of light will alter the law of enantiodromia in history, though we are often blinded to this fact by our knowledge. As she put it in *Everybody's Autobiography* (308), "if you have dim lights and you add another perhaps it makes it less light to your feeling than if you only have one dim one, if you have enough of them you are in total darkness anyway to your feeling."

She attaches it or in that way kneeling in a way in that way, in that way kneeling and being a chinese Christian meditatively. And there where there is water flowing there where she attaches it she attaches to it or she attaches it to it there where the water is flowing or kneeling there or beside it in a way of kneeling. —*Gertrude Stein,*
"Lend a Hand: Four Religions" (1922)

V. A WAY OF KNEELING

Beneath the social and technological crisis of our time it is not difficult to trace the outlines of a deepening spiritual crisis—a tendency to turn away from belief in an overarching divine government of the cosmos and to explore, in hope or despair, the capacities and responsibilities of man himself. For a good many years the most significant voices in philosophy and the arts have been those which have urged us to leave the shallows and surfaces of existence and plunge into the realized depths of this spiritual reorientation. It is in this general wave of thought and expression—or so it seems to me—that Gertrude Stein becomes most interesting to the contemporary reader.

She lived her adult life between the turn of the century and 1946—dying only a year after the fateful summer of Hiroshima and Nagasaki. The earlier years of the century had been years of intellectual excitement and ferment—when, in spite of the First World War and the disillusionments that followed it, the advent of the "new" was everywhere welcomed by the avant-garde with intoxicated enthusiasm. But no one can compare the period between 1900 and 1935 with the thirty-odd years after it without realizing that a kind of ice age is upon us. In spite of incredible prosperity (at least in certain favored areas) and a surge of revolutionary action among races and nations that have hitherto been suppressed, both the haves and the have-nots seem to be haunted by anxiety rather than impelled by hope and vision. The years since Dachau and Hiroshima have been years of cold tension and vague, ominous forebodings.

It would be accurate enough (though no doubt an oversimplification) to characterize the underlying spiritual experience of the present and recent past as an experience of "waiting" and of "absence." At the heart of Christian experience one finds such figures as Simone Weil "waiting for God" yet not expecting His arrival; in a wry, perverse fashion the same thought is expressed in *Waiting for Godot*. At quite another level, however, we must describe the frantic activity of our age and its air of almost limitless distraction as a kind of marking time. It is not necessarily waiting for "God"—or even for disaster: it is a more diffused experience of emptiness—of separation or alienation.

Such emptiness is frequently diagnosed as the absence of God—a profound alienation from what Paul Tillich has called the Ground of our Being. But the new theologians who proclaim that God is dead have managed to dramatize, rather crudely but effectively, the fact that the word "God" can never be given an intelligible meaning on which all human beings are willing to agree. Thus to understand what alienation is, we cannot wait until we agree on what we mean by "God" and "alienation from God." Nor do we need to. The experience of alienation comes home to us far more concretely today in terms of man's estrangement from his fellowmen, from nature, and from his own deepest being—the self.

It is true that alienation from other life and from the roots of life is a perpetual feature of human experience, by no means peculiar to the present crisis. Christian theologians are fairly convincing when they equate alienation with sin, another perpetual feature of experience: after all, it is impossible to be estranged from nature and our fellowmen unless somehow we ought to be related to them or united with them. Still, although alienation is without doubt a permanent aspect of the human condition, this state seems to be almost intolerably intensified in our time. Small wonder, then, that a great many twentieth-century writers and thinkers have been preoccupied with it. Even in those years of creative effort which ushered in the twentieth century with such a blaze of splendor, we find that anxiety and estrangement are major themes, in one way or another.

On the surface, at least, Gertrude Stein does not seem to have dealt with the theme to any significant degree, and the question arises as to just what she has to say to the reader who is thoroughly aware of the realities of the later twentieth century. It is obvious enough that she is historically important—unusually sensitive, intelligent, and persistent, but thoroughly representative of the break with tradition and the commitment to novelty and experimentation that characterized the first third of the century. It is equally obvious that after World War I she played a cultural role at once catalytic and constructive, not only accelerating the processes of change among members of the younger generation, but awakening and fostering the creative impulse in a good many of them. But though she is still mentioned with frequency in memoirs and in periodical essays on many topics, it is inevitable that the impact of her personal influence will decline and be forgotten before long. There remain, however, the writings themselves—and the meaning of her life and effort.

It must be said, I think, that as a developed personality Stein warrants that effort to comprehend which her most important works demand. Without resorting to any of the consoling overbeliefs that sustain the tender-minded, she looked long and with direct and penetrating honesty at the facts of nature and experience. Her own life, in its serene integrity, is an impressive witness to the value of what she has to say. As I pointed out in the opening chapter of this study, she knew the meaning of alienation and estrangement in her early years, perhaps more poignantly than most people do. But in spite of her long preoccupation with time and emergent novelty, her mature personality suggests the timeless harmony of an Eastern sage. Picasso saw and expressed this quality in his famous portrait of her; one sees it in the pyramidal solidity of the Jo Davidson statue; it appears in the later photographs, where the figure so matriarchal yet so sexless, the ageless head with its enigmatic eyes, are an irresistible reminder of the Buddha.

Thus without passing judgment on her place as a writer (or even as a thinker), we may come to suspect that, though hers is a thoroughly "secular" voice, it is one of the more authentic voices of the human spirit in the twentieth century. She herself would not have said the "human spirit": she was concerned, we have seen, with "being existing" and the "human mind." These phrases recall the opposition she always pointed out between human nature (locus of alienation and subject of most literature) and the human mind (a manifestation of the creativity in man as inexplicable, ultimately, as lightning, and a good deal more potent). It is apparently out of her realized experience of the human mind, of "being existing," that she bypasses the theme of alienation in most of her important writing and focuses largely on an experience that might be called reconciliation.

In an age of absence, in other words, she bears witness to "presence"—the presence of mystery and creativity in nature and in man. There is a sense in which her very preoccupations, including her almost casual assumption of the naturalistic viewpoint, attest to that estrangement of man from nature and the past which so well characterizes our time. But though in *Doctor Faustus Lights the Lights* she projects the image of alienation very vividly, she clearly suggests, as we have seen, a possible resolution of the difficulty. In an age of anxiety she affirms the fact that wholeness of experience is possible, Equally important, however, is the fact that in an era of propaganda, corrupted language, and the breakdown of communication she works for a language that has been purged of its unclean service to Mammon.

Nevertheless, just as Gertrude Stein's impressive though baffling personality can hardly be understood in terms of sanctity—or even in terms of Oriental "liberation"—so her expressions of harmony and presence must not be understood as revealing any traditional religious attitude, either Eastern or Western. Self-discipline and spiritual exercises may have made her a creative force. But it cannot be said too plainly that in cosmic vision, as well as in personal relationships, she was a singularly tough-minded realist. She was noted for her wit and gaiety and a deliberately prosaic quality of thought and perception; there was very little that was exalted in her language or in the feeling she expressed.

It seems fairly clear that the light, flat prosiness so characteristic of Stein's style is the product of her fundamental ascesis. In other words, it derives from the self-restraint of a writer who has chosen to address the possibility of the full human mind in her reader. Very early in her writing career, as we saw in Chapter Two, Gertrude Stein seems to have regarded the novel as a dead form; in fact she often advised young writers to write essays or "meditations," since neither character nor identity (insidious aspects of human nature) can be involved in meditation. For the human mind functions at the level of impersonality and a timeless, selfless absorption in reality for its own sake. This view carries with it not only a deep respect for the works of genius, but an almost equal respect for the reader, a respect based on the possibility of his response at the level of the human mind.

For Gertrude Stein, in other words, meditation is more than reflection: it is an act of presence—an act of communion with the ongoing reality around her—which is psychologically though not theologically akin to what Christian mystics have called "contemplation of the creatures." Only through such participation, she believed, will the word have life, and only through the written word can life be immortalized. The written word is the one medium in which all mediation disappears. Words on the printed page bear no resemblance to the things they signify, and they are therefore closed entirely to sense perception but open immediately to the inward eye. All other forms of expression create an object with extension in space or time that is a necessary part of them; they are bound by one or the other and therefore appeal to eye or ear. But through words the writer can commune in silence with an unknown reader, across space and time, by signs which in themselves need make no appeal to sense. Thus, paradoxically, the written word is the most immediate of all the modes of expression. In it the writer is disembodied but enduring. "Mention me if you can," Gertrude Stein said, "because I am here" (GHA, 155).

She also said, "How can a language alter. It does not it is an altar" (UK, 108). To eternalize in this way a fleeting moment of life is to create a new value from what would otherwise have been carried along in the temporal flux to oblivion. Such a value need never have been realized even fleetingly, of course, because there is no necessary relation between knower and known. To put it another way, the number of authentic poems or masterpieces of writing is of no importance, and no one of them has any necessity either to be or not to be. They are gratuitous acts of "presence" itself, witnesses to the freedom of the human mind in the face of the cosmos.

The act of realization essential to such creation is an exchange between two finalities—the human mind and the world in which it is a perennial possibility. No matter how trivial the created object may seem to be in terms of the world's work, the value of the interchange is infinite. But the authentic word serves no purpose beyond itself; its measure is devotion rather than use. In Gertrude Stein's vocabulary it is variously called a hymn, a prayer, a song, a meditation, or a masterpiece. She herself was committed to a rather limited, astringent mode of intellectual appeal, in the form of meditation with occasional elements of lyricism. Apparently she felt that in our time the dangers of manipulative suasion and ignoble appeals to "human nature" made authentic work with the great traditional forms and themes almost impossible. But her metaphysical theory of literature is undoubtedly based on the humanistic meaning of the masterpieces of the past.

In contrast to the written word, the spoken word is mediated both by the voice and by the physical presence of the speaker. Gertrude Stein found lecturing difficult because it brought her into contact with an audience. She sought to isolate herself in every way possible so that communication, a cheap and trivial substitute for shared insight and vision, would not interfere with communion. When a writer is writing, "that physical something by existing does not connect him with anything but concentrates him on recognition" (N, 56); when he is addressing, or writing for, an audience, that "physical something" diverts his energies and therefore may deprive his words of authenticity. Only insofar as the consciousness is concentrated upon its object—when it is "present" to it—can there be anything truly spoken or truly written. "By written I mean made. And by made I mean felt" (LIA, 165). And over and over again Stein defined the genius as the one who talks and listens at the same time. "One may really indeed say that that is the essence of genius, of being most intensely alive, that is being one who is at the same time talking and listening" (LIA, 170).

In this sense, obviously, talking and listening are not consecutive acts. They occur simultaneously, in concentration—"the two in one and the one in two"—"like the motor going inside the car and the car moving, they are part of the same thing" (LIA, 180, 170). These phrases are a vivid way of describing the artist's experience of intense ingatheredness, in which the object of thought or perception and his own deep "inner voice" are indistinguishable as they dictate the words. In such an act of presence all the dualisms are resolved: knower and known are joined in one object—the created poem, or masterpiece—through which they may become intelligible to the reader's intuition. Authentically created writing thus inevitably becomes ritual, the purpose being to invoke at one and the same moment the hidden reality of otherness and the hidden reality of creative insight, or the human mind.

Such a theory of creative writing rather clearly equates the work of genius with prayer and ritual, or the activity of saints; in the same way, it identifies the flash of creativity with the experience of grace. What may be less clear, however, is that this is also a theory of the relationship between writer and reader which has an important bearing on the problem of man's estrangement from his fellowman.

Gertrude Stein wrote little or nothing to suggest that she was directly concerned with this problem—at least at the level of personal relationships and social conflicts. But she obviously felt that all of humanity participates in some sense (though to a great extent feebly or merely potentially) in the human mind; and her insistence that writing requires a special sort of integrity implies that genuine understanding (the presence of mind to mind) among human beings may well be possible at this level alone. She achieved fame and a wide and appreciative public with her later, more comprehensible work. Yet she never watered down her austere demand upon the reader's wholeness of response. Moreover, in her advice to writers, who after all are the "saints" in this communion, she makes an even more absolute and rigorous demand. Writing is sacred, and she frequently warns the writer against trying to serve two masters:

When I say god and mammon concerning the writer writing, I mean that any one can use words to say something. And in using these words to say what he has to say he may use words directly or indirectly. If he uses these words indirectly he says what he intends to have heard by somebody who is to hear and in so doing inevitably he has to serve mammon. Mammon may be a success, mammon may be an effort he is to produce, mammon may be a pleasure he has from hearing what he himself has done, mammon may be his way of explaining, mammon may be a laziness that needs nothing but going on, in short mammon may be anything done indirectly. Now serving god for a writer who is writing is writing anything directly, it makes no difference what it is but it must be direct, the relation between the thing done and the doer must be direct. (LIA, 23-24)

Only at this level also, it would seem, is there a direct relation between one mind and another mind—that is, only when the reader is absorbed in re-experiencing the original absorption of the writer. This is an experience that transcends time, as anyone knows who has brooded over an insight in Plato, or a fragment of a Sophoclean chorus, or a scene in Homer; and it is also an experience of concentrated attention on something that has nothing whatever to do with the claims and passions of the ego. There is a characteristic homeliness and humor in Gertrude Stein's favorite illustration of the nature of this experience. It resembles, she says, the moment when Robinson Crusoe discovers Friday's footprints, a moment that "is one of the most perfect examples of the non-existence of time and identity which makes a masterpiece" (WAM, 93). For like Crusoe in his dramatic confrontation of the "otherness" in the world, the artist, the saint, or the philosopher—or the reader who is caught up in the enchantment of reading—becomes most truly himself, precisely in this moment of self-forgetfulness. It was to this paradox that Gertrude Stein pointed when she said that "the human mind is like not being in danger but being killed" (GHA, 28), and that "At any moment when you are you you are you without the memory of yourself because if you remember yourself while you are you you are not for purposes of creating you" (WAM, 85-86).

As readers we cease to be passive consumers and become

self-creators in those moments of absorbed self-recollection and self-forgetting. Such continuity of insight and deepened awareness of what is essential to the "human" is of course the sole defense that can be offered for literature, in a computerizing age when even the writers themselves have begun to question the function and future of their art. This is the first time in human history when such a defense has needed to be made. It is not a problem that Gertrude Stein had any occasion to consider, but with what looks like prophetic insight she suggested an answer. That is to say, she reminds the aspiring artist of the nature of authentic creativity. Only in repeated acts of selfless concentration—and selfless recognition of the otherness he faces—can the writer find direct words to awaken insight in his readers. Furthermore, by inplication at least, it is only on the basis of self-forgetting encounters with one another that human beings can rise above their predatory or manipulative human nature and arrive at even a partial meeting of minds, a partial thawing out of their estrangement.

As a writer Gertrude Stein was not concerned with discussing the ethical and psychological aspects of encounter and dialogue and the I-Thou relationship. Selfless absorption in another personality she was capable of, as an artist: her capacity for this kind of attention was not limited to objects and landscapes, and from her method in writing portraits it is clear that she knew how to talk and listen at the same time where people were concerned. From the beginning she was looking for the "bottom nature" in her sitters, and looking with an unusual degree of sympathetic vibration. Undoubtedly, too, she knew that genuine love and friendship know how to listen in this way—and not only to make a portrait. She also knew that modern man's alienation from his fellows is revealed most strikingly in his usual incapacity for such listening. In fact she treats this theme in some of her early portraits, notably in *Two: Gertrude Stein and Her Brother*. But it seems to me that she also focuses upon the root cause of the ailment—man's fundamental alienation from himself; rather, to put it more precisely, she is concerned with the way to heal this alienation.

In other words, Stein most resembles the sages of tradition in her arduous, heroic effort to effect a breakthrough to the buried genius she was determined to become. All human beings are born, it seems, with one fundamental built-in form of alienation: unless a heroic attempt is made to turn inward, the surface self or ego is almost wholly unaware of the otherness within—the stranger who may first appear as enemy but finally becomes both helper and friend. The effort to tap one's own deeper resources is therefore always a quest for self-knowledge and self-unification. There can be little doubt that Gertrude Stein was at least partially successful in this quest. As we saw in Chapter Three, however, it was in pursuit of a rather less impressive goal—the "new word" to express a cubistic vision of household objects—that she seems to have stumbled almost by accident onto the time-honored method of arriving at selfhood.

Whether one calls it contemplation or recollection or yogic concentration, this technique of disciplined waiting and intent yet passive listening was apparently the source of Gertrude Stein's linguistic practice as well as the inspiration of her theory of creativity, "being existing" and the human mind. But to people who find yoga and kindred subjects interesting, the odd thing about Stein's long habit of spiritual exercises is that they were focused—by her own account, at least—on trivial or evanescent objects. Her cosmic vision is one of temporal flux and vanishing: there is no sense here of eternal meaning or purpose, no goal beyond the present moment. Her present moment, in fact, is not obviously identifiable with the "eternal now" of the mystics. Thus, in a lifetime of effort and disciplined attention, what she sought to realize was succession, on the one hand, and a kind of abstract universality on the other. What she tried to express was the shifting scenes and objects arbitrarily selected for attention, or to construct out of the chance concatenation of objects in any moment, a "composition." She wanted to convey the essential nature of living creatures or of objects moving in space, and by the intensity of her own mental activity to project motion into still lifes. Some of her most disconcerting compositions are those relying heavily upon repetition: "As I said if you like, it was like a cinema picture made up of succession and each moment having its own emphasis that is its own difference and so there was the moving and the existence of each moment as it was in me" (LIA, 198). Most of the spiritual masters of East and West alike have realized the self in a spirit of religious dedication to the divine—or at the very least, as in Hinayana Buddhism, in a spirit of universal compassion and a desire to lead sufferers out of nature and the cosmos and into the Clear Void. But Gertrude Stein traveled light, rejecting all such aims as well as all religious formulations.

Thus she was always careful to distinguish between the truth of metaphor and the truth of fact, pointing out, for example, when she compared creativity to the service of

God, that she did not mean religion in any sense "excepting the need to complete that which is trying to fill itself up inside anyone" (LIA, 19). She insisted that her writings had an intellectual, not a mystical, basis. She also liked to say, however, that she was superstitious—her way of pointing toward the irrational beliefs that seemed "true" to her. Concerning her meditations upon American religion Thornton Wilder writes that she was "tracking down certain irrational ways we have of knowing things, of believing things, and of being governed by these ways of believing" (FIA, xvi). But for her the essential mystery, baffling to reason even when not productive of irrationality, is the contradiction in man between infinite and finite. Perhaps her most succinct account of man's "religious" predicament occurs in the following passage:

After all one is brought up not a Christian but in Christian thinking and I can remember being excited when I first read the Old Testament to see that there was no future life and I found how naturally that worried me, that there is no limit to space and yet one is living in a limited space and inside oneself there is no sense of time but actually one is always living in time, and there is the will to live but really when one is completely wise that is when one is a genius the things that make you a genius make you live but have nothing to do with being living that is with the struggle for existence. (EA, 243)

In these remarks, made in the 1930s, there is more than a hint that Stein thought of herself as a genius. But at the outset of her career she had not been a genius (at least not in the sense of being "completely wise"). It would seem that at some point the breakthrough was successful—a fact that one might surmise also from her long preoccupation with the nature and locus of human creativity. Furthermore, it is evident from her frequent association of artistic creativity with prayer that writing had given her an experience which required a religious vocabulary to express it. For a writer whose compositions seem grounded in concern for trivia, in fact, she refers very often to religion, though she expresses her ideas in metaphors and paradoxes. Donald Sutherland says that she wrote so frequently of saints because they "afforded her a stable metaphor on which to maintain her own generically poetic exaltation, her own vision of a world saturated with miracles." [1] But the chief miracle was evidently the self-creation of a poet and the discovery of her own creativity—her deeper Self, the ultimate source of wisdom.

As we saw in Chapter Three, this was a miracle patiently fostered by repeated small acts of self-discipline and directed attention. Perhaps she had been inspired by the heady mysticism inherent in the doctrines of cubism and other avant-garde movements of the decade before World War I. No doubt, too, she owed some of her faith in contemplation to her acquaintance with the thought of Bergson and William James. But as James Feibleman suggests in the following passage, she probably made her beginning in the search for a "tiny but real affair" that she could think of as her own:

Did not Wittgenstein, Paul Klee, and Gertrude Stein employ the same method in philosophy, in painting, and in literature, respectively? Just what this common method is was best stated perhaps in its most general terms by Klee: "It is a great handicap and a great necessity to have to start with the smallest. I want to be as though new born, knowing nothing absolutely about

1. Sutherland, *Gertrude Stein*, p. 124.

Europe; ignoring poets and fashions, to be almost primitive. Then I want to do something very modest; to work out by myself a tiny, formal motif, one that my pencil will be able to hold without any technique. One favorable moment is enough. The little thing is easily and concisely set down. It's already done! It is a tiny but real affair, and some day, through the repetition of such small but original deeds, there will come one work upon which I can really build." [2]

For Gertrude Stein, as I have suggested, the "one work" upon which to build was *Tender Buttons*—mandala and reconciling image and, as she herself admitted, "very good poetry." My view of *Tender Buttons* as a mandala is echoed both by Feibleman's association of Stein with Paul Klee in the above passage and by an equally interesting comment of Sir Herbert Read's. In *The Forms of Things Unknown* Read observes that we contemplate a work of art "not to escape from ourselves . . . but to be reconciled with ourselves and with the absurdity of existence." In the world of modern painting he finds such images of reconciliation in the works of Kandinsky, Picasso, Klee, Mondrian, Gabo, and Moore, which he divides into two groups. One group is "abstract in the sense that they do not represent the sense-data of normal modes of perception"; these, "formless and discordant," are produced by arbitrary methods, often without the intervention of the conscious will. A second group of paintings by the same men he classifies as true mandalas—"images of wholeness and integration." But regardless of method, Read suggests, all of these artists have been seeking to pass beyond

2. James Feibleman, *Inside the Great Mirror* (The Hague: Martin Nijhoff, 1958), p. 205.

consciousness in order to be carried (as Erich Neumann put it), "backward to an all-embracing participation with the world."

In saying that *Tender Buttons* is a mandala, then, one need not deny or even underestimate the importance of modern painting in the development of Gertrude Stein. She shared the methods and purposes of such men as Klee and Picasso, but such methods and purposes were rather more profound than many Stein critics have acknowledged. In any case, when *Tender Buttons* is read "in depth," with its murmured echoes of the great archetypes of light and vision, growth and the sacred enclosure, it must be regarded as a reconciling image—a title that Read is unwilling to confer upon Joyce's *Ulysses* or Eliot's later poems. Eliot, he thinks, "tried perhaps too deliberately to reanimate ancient symbols rather than create new ones." [3]

Let us ignore the question whether it is ever possible for an individual artist to create a symbol that is completely new in the sense Read implies. In actual fact a reconciling image exists not only to bring together unconscious depths and conscious purpose, but to reunite what is most ancient, primitive, and traditional with what is as new and unpredictable as tomorrow. When *Tender Buttons* is even partially considered in this light, it seems to effect exactly this kind of reconciliation: cubistic dislocations unite to suggest archetypes of natural growth, and, although the murmured suggestions are ancient, the total image is modern in its simplicity. For here is the image of a lived-in house—but

3. Herbert Read, *The Forms of Things Unknown* (New York: Horizon Press, 1960), pp. 196-197.

this is symbolic, in both literature and dream, of the self at home in its body; and here is a green, watered garden—again, symbolic of a woman's body, of a life well ordered, of a mind in harmony with its natural surroundings and its work.

In other words everything in *Tender Buttons* suggests (at a pretty well-concealed level, it is true) not only the thrust of nascent creativity from the depths, but a profound agreement between the emerging new self and nature. The great GHAR roots from which the mandala seems to evolve carry intimations, as we have seen, of the numinous origins of language, of ritual dancing in a sacred enclosure, of the ritual character of all authentic writing. But these miracles of language, ceremony, and realized selfhood are not alien to the miracle celebrated in the title itself—with its overtones of a garden and burgeoning growth. This reconciling image speaks not only of the integrated self but of its participation in the order of nature.

As Read has suggested, this kind of participation was the goal of a small company of great painters and sculptors, most of whose purposes and method were shared by Gertrude Stein. This group of artists was keenly aware of the coming mechanization of man. Perhaps this was because they felt both the forms and the new meanings of the airplane and the motion picture, as well as the landscapes of height and succession they confer upon us, even before these early inventions had matured. Perhaps, too, the mental landscape of the time had rendered forever inaccessible the old half-mythic modes of communing with nature which were natural to the romantics of the nineteenth century. In any case, many of these men of the early twentieth century seem to have known that no artist could bear and recreate the shattering burden of the coming era unless he had made the heroic inward journey "into the self."

There can be no attempt here to assess the achievement, whether technical or spiritual, of the cubists and other non-representational painters and sculptors of that period. What is most interesting is that, as the best of them saw it, the creative act had to be a union of the technical and the spiritual in one act—however small that act might be. This is the very essence of the long effort and discipline of Gertrude Stein. A work executed in this spirit may turn out to be a mandala (whether by unconscious guidance or partly conscious purpose is unimportant), if the artist's need for deeper exploration is still great. And since the mandala is an instrument for invoking and unifying the self—as well as reconciling it with its labors and its materials—we might well expect a kind of triumphant harmony in the later work of those artists who have created reconciling images.

This is in fact what we find in the more purely aesthetic compositions of Gertrude Stein, in the years following *Tender Buttons*. There is audible in much of her work a note of singing—as if she were aware of a divine chorus and her own inevitable part in it. Perhaps this concept of the "chorus" was one of her semantic discoveries while writing *Tender Buttons*. But no matter what her subject matter was—and as she became more playful in tone, she wrote more and more frequently about "saints and singing"—she was never solemn or conventionally religious. She had wit and a love of the comic; since her object was only to be present both to her writing and to her reader, she gives the impression of child-like intentness, as if she were concentrating upon each movement in an absorbing game. Her work is filled with a feeling of delight and freedom from care, even when she is describing the wars she has seen. She wrote without tears, about something hard to name:

Dogs and birds and a chorus and a flat land.

How do you like what you are. The bird knows, the dogs know and the chorus well the chorus yes the chorus if the chorus which is the chorus.

The flat land is not the chorus.

Human nature is not the chorus.

The human mind is not the chorus.

Perspiration is not the chorus.

Tears are not the chorus.

Food is not the chorus.

Money is not the chorus.

What is the chorus. (GHA, 76)

For Gertrude Stein there is a harmony between man and the universe, but it is not a heavenly harmony—not the music of the spheres. It is not a process in time or a result of progress or an event in history. It is perhaps "the choir invisible of those immortal dead who live again" [4] in masterpieces, who are present to the world and to themselves, participating in experience, contemplating it, loving it, dreaming about it, and expressing it in the forms of art. She rejected all forms of mysticism, theology, or systematic philosophy which would place the harmony of things beyond experience. The chorus as she conceived it is a harmony of separate and distinct voices—not a transcendent or an immanent paean in which the many are resolved into the One.

So there is little exalted rhetoric in her writing. But there is a great deal of joy—in the pleasures of perception, of

4. Stein quotes George Eliot in *Everybody's Autobiography* (116).

imagination, of play and song. When one lives consciously in the actual present, one is "doing nothing" in exactly the way saints are "doing nothing" when they pray or sing or perform their ritual tasks. The song is intent and serious only in the attention devoted to it. It asks for nothing, but finds everything. "They liked it as much as they ever liked it before because the wind blew and blew the birds about and they liked it they liked it as much when the wind did that" (GHA, 92-93).

Edmund Wilson once wrote of Gertrude Stein as "registering the vibrations of a psychological country like some august seismograph whose charts we haven't the training to read." [5] But in spite of the psychological mechanism that registers them, the truth is rather that those vibrations are spiritual, having to do with the longing for unity and harmony and a strenuous effort to achieve these ends. That this was Gertrude Stein's concern is suggested by a certain painful crisis she endured in the later part of her career.

Before the American tour she had always identified herself with her work. Then publicity had suddenly forced her to assume a new role, a persona that was an excerpt of the external world. Back in Bilignin, in the summer of 1935, she was unable to regain contact with the deeper layers of her own mind: "Nothing inside me needed to be written. Nothing needed any word and there was no word inside me that could not be spoken and so there was no word inside me" (EA, 64). Confronted by this feeling of emptiness, she meditated upon identity, memory, and eternity. Her own past was no longer real: the places she had lived in had been

5. *Axel's Castle,* p. 253.

metamorphosed in the course of the years and existed only as memories, and the child she had been no longer returned her gaze from the mirror. Thus she faced, in its most painful because least creative form, the question, "What am I?" Without doubt this experience of desolation led her of necessity to the composition of two important works—both of which help to give conceptual clarification to the continuity of her work.

When life loses its meaning and the soul is aware of its sickness, the alternatives are breakdown or a fresh and perhaps deeper look at oneself and reality. When there is no other way to re-enter the lost "garden," it is possible, as many have realized, to dig one's way back in by sustained reflection and intellectual understanding. No one as courageous and persistent as Gertrude Stein could have taken a psychic setback in the spirit of defeat: she knew too well the role of will power, reflection, and repeated effort in the creation of "masterpieces"—especially the supreme masterpiece of inner realization. *The Geographical History of America* is therefore in some ways her crowning achievement. A triumph of lost ground regained, it is as full of wit, song, and gaiety as anything she ever wrote; but it is also, despite the minor difficulties involved in reading it, a coherent expression of her special metaphysical vision.

The experience of self-division and crisis was evidently also the basis for *Doctor Faustus Lights the Lights.* As we have seen, this curious work may be understood as a symbol of the failure of science and the purely intellectual outlook to confer meaning and joy upon experience. It is also a paradigm of that widespread ailment of our time—the collapse or partial disintegration of the successful and apparently

211 WAY OF KNEELING

well-integrated personality on the threshold of its autumnal years. It dramatizes a common cause of this ailment—the rebellion of the buried psychic functions against the over-developed but ultimately sterile intellect, which has dom-inated life too long. Gertrude Stein understood very well, I think, the experience of self-alienation presented here. Again, as in *Tender Buttons,* the "villain" is the ego. There she had written, "Act so that there is no use in a centre." In *Doctor Faustus*, it is Faust's ego that is sent to hell. Thus, in both compositions, reconciliation is achieved through ego trans-cendence. The power of the Jungian symbols to express dynamically the truth of modern man's predicament and its solution must have led her at last, after thirty years of non-symbolic writing, to acknowledge the occasional value of symbolism in art, as Picasso had already done in his *Minotauromachy* (1935) and *Guernica* (1937).

Gertrude Stein's preoccupation with the achievement of true selfhood runs like an underground river beneath her visible works. She is "representative" of our times partly be-cause she was not a person of great genius to begin with and partly because she was burdened, at the outset, with familiar conflicts and tensions and jerry-built compromise "integra-tions." Most important of all, perhaps, is the fact that she felt so keenly the need for sacred experience in a world that is secular in more than one way—temporal and evanescent as all its values and creations seem to be. Committed to her time's rejection of tradition, yet disgusted with its slick and meaningless clichés, she found in the deepest levels of her own being a passion for communion, "presence," and the sacred word. But because of her commitment to the current

world view of natural science, she found it impossible to believe in any all-embracing divine order, either personal or
impersonal. This too is a dilemma that has frustrated and
sometimes tortured a great many of the most sensitive and
intelligent men and women of this century.

Apparently she resolved the dilemma for herself by means
of a kind of vatic art, suggesting a personal experience of
harmony that in our time seems incommunicable. But the
very unintelligibility and dislocations of such writing provide a magnifying glass for language itself—a glass that
forces the reader to look again, and much more carefully
and honestly than he has looked before, at every ordinary
word. She always seems to be saying, therefore, often almost
inadvertently but sometimes quite deliberately, that until we
have cleansed the doors of perception and common speech,
we have not earned the right to speak to one another of
anything very profound.

Behind the fresh honesty of her language, however, we
find a world view that is not only coherent but profound.
When we consider her metaphysical vision of reality, coupled
with her long practice of "spiritual exercises," Gertrude Stein
ceases to be merely a representative phenomenon of her
time. In theory and practice alike she speaks to the modern
consciousness with a kind of hard-earned, astringent wisdom
which, though stripped of all consoling "overbeliefs" and
focused wholly upon the present moment of experience, is
an irreducible condensation of the spirituality of the past.
Her primary object is not to explain the cosmic creativity but
to elucidate and evoke in others the groundless act of presence—an act by which a man may realize at one stroke his
own "human mind" and the beauty or meaning of some

aspect of the cosmos. In this philosophy, authentic "being existing" depends wholly on one thing—the selfless realization of the human mind in an act of freedom.

There is an interesting analogy between this view and that of some of the great religions of tradition—notably Buddhism. But Gertrude Stein did not take the final step of believing in an eternal and pervasive spiritual reality, since to believe that "being existing" is in the traditional sense eternal and omnipresent is to believe that all creatures must come to it at last—an act of faith in the supremacy of spirit of which she was utterly incapable. A thoroughgoing temporalist, she saw and felt as final the evanescence of all individual forms. Although she resembles Whitehead in supposing that creativity is everlasting, the recurrent miracles of "being existing" with which the world is saturated are apparently discrete realizations. Like William James, in fact, she seems to have believed in a multiverse rather than a genuine universe. Since something very like this view is probably today shared by a great many people, it may well be that only her kind of strict empiricism has any spiritual message for the disenchanted secular mind.

The real message is all the more impressive for being demonstrated in action and practice, not in verbal discussion. It might be noted here how much Gertrude Stein resembles the teachers of Zen Buddhism—in her predilection for jokes and riddles, in her matter-of-fact language and fondness for non sequiturs and sudden absurdities, in the playfulness that got her a reputation, in certain quarters, for being a mountebank, and in her pursuit of the creative act that would be both technically "without any technique" (because beyond it) and spiritual at the same time. She

and such painters as Paul Klee were intuitively close in this
regard to those Zen masters of swordsmanship, archery, and
painting who found the experience of ultimate reality in concentrating on their craft with increasing devotion. But
nowhere is she so much in the true spirit of Zen as in her
method of suggesting, but never actually stating, the true
nature of the goal she reached throughout her long period
of concentration.

Feibleman has linked her with Wittgenstein as well as
with Klee because they all share, he thinks, a common
method. Like the Zen masters, and like Wittgenstein, Stein
seems to be urging the reader to discover something for himself that can never be really said. The *Tractatus Logico-
Philosophicus* closes with the following explanation of "the
only strictly correct philosophical method":

My propositions are elucidatory in this way: he who understands me finally recognizes them as senseless, when he has
climbed out through them, on them, over them. (He must so to
speak throw away the ladder, after he has climbed up on it.)

He must surmount these propositions: then he sees the world
rightly. (6.54)

Whereof one cannot speak, thereof one must be silent. (7.0)

INDEX

INDEX